PRIME MOVER OF NEW INDIA

NARENDRA MODI

DR. PRATIK UMREY

Dedicated To The People Of India

Contents

Foreword

In Historic General Elections of 2014,India elected its leader with an absolute majority to fulfill the aspirations of 1.25 billion Indians. On 26th May, 2014 when Narendra Modi took oath as the 14th Prime Minister of India, he had millions of eyes full of hope looking towards him for their bright future. He was expected to begin a new regime of governance in the country. As the leader of the world's largest democracy Modi was aware of the expectations from his government and was determined to live upto the expectations.The vision of Prime Minister Modi is to build a New India by fulfilling the dreams of 1.25 billion Indians. Every second of his life is devoted to the service of the country. He has brought the derailed economy on right track and now the atmosphere in the country is optimistic. International community is confident that India is emerging in the leadership of PM Modi. This book also includes glimpse of political journey of Narendra Modi from being a Grassroot Worker Of BJP to becoming one of the most powerful prime ministers of India.This book provides a detailed look at India's transformation And BJP'S transformation under PM Modi's visionary leadership .Changes From welfare to culture, from ease of doing business to national security, from economic growth to ease of living, The book discusses various Initiatives taken by Prime minister Narendra Modi In Contribution Towards New India.

PREFACE

Dr. Pratik Umrey Served As Alderman Of BJP At Municipal Corporation,Durg Chhattisgarh,He Was youngest Alderman of Chhattisgarh,His Age is 31 years.He is Member Of Bhartiya Janta Party since 2008 And was also Former vice President Of Bhartiya Janta yuva Morcha Durg. He has closely followed the evolution and rise of the Bharatiya Janta Party Himself.He is Author of Five Other books And Is First Author of Chhattisgarh who has written both fiction & Nonfiction genre.

"We do not run the government on whims of an individual, our progress is reforms driven, our reforms are policy driven and our policies are people driven."- PM Modi

I
Overview

The Bharatiya Janata Party (BJP) government at the Centre completes its successful eight years under the dynamic and decisive leadership of Prime Minister (PM) Narendra Modi. The last eight years have been a trendsetter for India. The nation has moved from the politics of casteism, dynasty, corruption and appeasement to the politics of development, growth, unity and nationalism.

This remarkable journey has strengthened democracy in its real sense by empowering the marginalised sections of our society — from poor and backward classes, Dalits and minorities, tribals and oppressed classes to women and youth. It has also been a journey of changing the Indian psyche — from "nothing is possible in this country" to "everything is possible if the government and the people have the will and commitment". The commitment of 1.35 billion Indians towards the vision of PM Modi reflects on the ground. It also proves that if a leader has a policy and programme, intention and dedication, every challenge can be addressed, every problem can be solved.

The nation has not just changed under the leadership of PM Modi, but a new chapter of remarkable growth and fast-paced development is also being written. Today, eight years of changing India reflects in every Indian's eyes. In the last eight years, our poverty rate reduced from 22% to 10%, and extreme poverty fell below 1% and remained static at 0.8%. Our per capita income doubled while foreign reserves also increased two-fold. In the past 70 years, only 637,000 primary schools were constructed, but under the Modi government, 653,000 schools have been built so far. Under this government, 15 new All India Institutes of Medical Sciences were sanctioned, out of which 10 have become operational and five are in advanced stages of construction. The number of doctors jumped by 1.2 million. India created the second largest road network in the world, and our solar and wind power generation capacity doubled in the past five years.

Year after year, India broke records in food grain production. In 2012-13 our food grain production was 255 million tonnes, which increased to 316.06 million tonnes in 2021-22, the highest ever in our history. Despite the global economic slowdown due to the Covid-19 pandemic, India managed to clock a record in merchandise exports at $418 billion in the last financial year. Under the Modi government, new benchmarks were set. As India battled the pandemic, it was PM Modi who led from the front. He gave India not one but two "Made in India" vaccines, and opened government coffers to provide free rations to over 800 million Indians for the past two years at an expenditure of ₹3.40 lakh crore.

There are several firsts associated with the last eight years. The common man got free medical insurance coverage through Ayushman Bharat Yojna, while farmers and labourers got a monthly pension. For the first time, farmers started getting the benefit of the Kisan Samman Nidhi for farming purposes, and it was our government that formed a policy for organic farming.

Then there are several path breaking schemes — Jan Dhan Yojana, Ujjwala Yojana, Kisan Samman Nidhi, Ayushman Bharat Yojana, Gareeb Kalyan Yojana, Swachh Bharat Yojana, Awas Yojana, Jal Jivan Mission, Digital India, Gram Vikas Yojana, Goods and Services Tax — which not only empowered citizens but also strengthened our economy and made India resilient and self-reliant. Schemes such as Atmanirbhar Bharat, Vocal for Local, Gati Shakti Yojana, PLI (production linked incentive) catapulted India to the top of the global world order.

In previous regimes, the willpower to deal with perennial problems was lacking and everything was left to fate. PM Modi's innovative and decisive approach in dealing with problems made all the difference. His firm resolve led to the scrapping of Article 370, construction of the grand Ram Temple in Ayodhya, abolition of instant triple talaq, passing of the Citizenship Amendment Act and surgical strikes on terror camps across the border. His unique style led to the identification of 1,800 old laws which had become redundant, and the scrapping of 1,450 of them. No previous government had thought of this. This made lives simpler for citizens and improved government efficiency.

Foreign policy is one field where India has excelled under PM Modi. From Iraq, Yemen, Afghanistan to Ukraine, India showed the world how effective foreign relations help in saving the lives of citizens. India also led from the front when it came to the issues of terrorism, global warming, Global Solar Alliance, effectiveness of Quad and our strong relations with our neighbours. These eight years were also a period of India's cultural resurgence. Yoga and Ayurveda caught the world's attention, and India's lost cultural and religious icons regained their glory, including the transformation of our holiest places such as Kashi Vishwanath Dham and Kedarnath Dham.

Under PM Modi, the BJP broke records and reached new heights. Today, the BJP is the world's biggest political organisation with 180 million members. In 2014, the BJP and its allies had governments in seven states, today we have our governments in 18. For the first time, the BJP crossed the 100-mark in the Rajya Sabha and broke electoral records in Uttar Pradesh, Uttarakhand, Assam, Goa, Manipur and Tripura.

The secret behind the BJP's success under PM Modi is the trust and blessings of Indians that our party won. People today know that there is a government at the Centre that works for their welfare and is committed to Sabka Saath, Sabka Vikas, Sabka Vishwas, Sabka Prayas.

Under PM Modi, the BJP is committed to transform India, make India a country where all are one, all are happy and prosperous. It is time again to take a pledge to work hard and commit ourselves to make India a happy and prosperous nation.....

(J.P Nadda)Bjp President

II

Glimpse of Prime Minister Narendra modi political carrier

Narendra Damodardas Modi was the first prime minister to be born in independent India -- on September 17, 1950 -- at Vadnagar, a small town in Mehsana district of North Gujarat. As he celebrates his 69th birthday on Tuesday, let's look at some of the milestones he crossed in his political career

1965: PM Narendra Modi began his political career as the Kankaria ward secretary of the Jan Sangh in 1965 in Ahmedabad.

1972: Narendra Modi joined the pro-Hindu group Rashtriya Swayamsevak Sangh (RSS) and set up a unit of the RSS's students' wing, the Akhil Bharatiya Vidyarthi Parishad. During his period there, he led the Navnirman anti-corruption agitation in 1974. He was also appointed as general secretary of an RSS committee - Gujarat Lok Sangharsh Samiti - coordinating opposition to the Emergency in Gujarat.

1987: Modi entered mainstream politics joining BJP in 1987, and was promoted as the General Secretary of the Gujarat unit within a year. He was also a prt of the coalition government BJP had formed for a brief period in 1990. He organised the Somnath to Ayodhya Rath Yatra of the then BJP chief L K Advani and the march from Kanyakumari to Kashmir, between 1988 and 1995.

1995: BJP came to power individually in Gujarat in 1995 and has its stronghold there ever since. Modi was appointed as the National Secretary of the party then. He was elevated to the post of General Secretary in 1998, and held the position till 2001...

2001: Probably the biggest shift to power for the BJP leader was when he was chosen to replace Gujarat's then Chief Minister Keshubhai Patel in 2001 since the latter's health was deteriorating. He was appointed by the then Prime Minister Atal Bihari Vajpayee. Modi had previously refused to be the deputy chief minister.

Modi swore in as the chief minister on October 7, 2001. He was elected to power in a by-poll on February 24, 2002.

2002: On February 27, 2002, a train, carrying Hindu pilgrims travelling from Ayodhya after performing a ceremony at the demolished Babri Masjid site, was set ablaze in Godhra. The fire killed hundreds of both Hindus and Muslims. Cases were filed against Modi over his alleged personal involvement in the incident. They were later closed by the Supreme Court as a Special Investigation Team (SIT) sited lack of evidence. The United Kingdom criticised his role in the riots in 2002, and Modi was even denied a diplomatic visa by the United States of America in 2005 citing his alleged involvement.

2002-2012: Narendra Modi had taken the Gujarat elections by a landslide with 127 of the 182 seats in the December 2002 Legislative Assembly elections, 117 in 20017 and 115 in 2012. He was lauded for his development model, with industries and business booming in Gujarat and also its economic development during his tenure as CM.

2014: Modi established himself as a prime ministerial candidate by 2014 General Elections. He even won a Time magazine reader's poll and was voted the person of the year in 2014. With "Ab ki bar Modi Sarkar" as the slogan, BJP campaigned far and wide for Modi. BJP eventually became the first party to win majority number of seats of 282 in the Lok Sabha polls, with Modi himself winning in both his constituencies - Vadodara and Varanasi.

2014-2019: Prime Minister Narendra Modi travelled to multiple countries to build socio-economic relations. In 2015, he made a surprise visit to Pakistan and met the then Pakistan Prime Minister Nawaz Sharif. He is the first Indian Prime Minister to visit Israel. He brought grand economic reforms such as the banning of all Rs 500 and 1000 notes on November 8, 2016, and the introduction of 'one nation, one tax' concept with GST on July 1, 2017.

2019: The 2019 general elections were once again in favour of 'Modi sarkar' as the NDA coalition had won a whopping 353 seats in the 543-member Parliament. Modi had also won his Varanasi constituency. Narendra Modi took oath as the Prime Minister of India for the second term in the presence of some 800 delegates from India and abroad on May 30, 2019. The abrogation of Article 370, criminalisation of Triple Talaq rule and the anti-terror law were a few of the changes that were implemented within the first 100 days of his tenure.

Rise of Narendra Modi

Spread across the country, committed to the RSS way, its Hindutva ideology, mostly celibates, disciplined cultural nationalists who have committed themselves "full-time" to the cause of social service and spreading the RSS mantra. They also strictly stay away from politics and political power, contributing only when "loaned" to affiliate bodies such as the BJP, for organisation work.

This is the quintessential, low-profile RSS pracharak, a committed ideologue with excellent organisational and peoplemanagement skills, who assumes the post of sangathan mantri (general secretary, organisation) when deputed to the BJP. Few have deviated from the path. Prime Minister Narendra Modi is one of them-a sangathan mantri who expressed a desire to stay in politics and was given a rare exemption.

Decades ago, the RSS first loaned pracharaks to help get the Bharatiya Jan Sangh running. Deendayal Upadhyaya was the most high-profile pracharak loaned to Syama Prasad Mookerjee in the Jan Sangh. The system of RSS men manning the organisational (sangathan) task in the party has since continued in the BJP. But with Modi in power, the demand for them has surged, obviously because of a meeting of political culture and style.

Not only are they more visible in and central to the political manoeuvres of the BJP as it pushes to consolidate its hold over power and spread its wings in new states, they have also formally taken power and become ministers, and in one case, chief minister. For Modi and BJP President Amit Shah, the tribe of pracharaks-cum-sangathan mantris has been the lot to tap into in their political climb to Delhi and now beyond. And with good reason-sangathan mantris are those rare leaders who are privy to deliberations within the party and the RSS.

In the BJP, the sangathan mantri attends the parliamentary board meeting and gets invited to all major RSS meetings. As a result, he knows the mind of the political outfit as well as its ideological parent on the issue of the day. The RSS nominates at least one of its pracharaks as sangathan mantri to each of its three dozen-plus affiliate organisations. In mass organisations such as the BJP, these sangathan mantris work under the radar, proving to be a reliable and dedicated hand to a mass leader. And on the rare occasion, they become visible, recognised faces. There is little doubt about their clout in the saffron family.

From selling tea at an obscure railway station to becoming the longest-serving Chief Minister of Gujarat and the poster-boy of BJP's strident Hindutva ideology, Narendra Damodardas Modi has proved to be an astute strategist.

The former RSS pracharak retained the reins of Gujarat as Chief Minister overcoming anti-incumbency, a united opposition onslaught and rebellion against his leadership from within BJP.

What distinguishes Modi from others is his art to exploit the situations, be it the devastation that came in the form of the earthquake of 2001 and the Godhra carnage a year later.

A radical brand of Hindutva has always been at the core of political discourse and he returned to it at the first first opportunity. This was evident in recent Gujarat poll campaign which he had begun by dwelling on issues of development and then switched to Hindutva, fired by Congress chief Sonia Gandhi's "merchant of death" remarks.

Over the last six years, he emerged as the most charismatic BJP leader in Gujarat who could sway the crowd through his championing the aggressive Hindutva.

Born in a Ghanchi community, which belongs to Other Backward Castes (OBC) family on September 17, 1950, Modi completed his schooling in Vadnagar and did his masters degree in political science from Gujarat University in 1980s while being a RSS pracharak.

Modi's leadership qualities showed in the early days of his student life when he became the student leader of Akhil Bharatiya Vidhyarthi Parishad.

Modi entered politics in 1987 by joining BJP. Within a year, he was elevated to the level of General Secretary of Gujarat unit of the party.

However, after the split in BJP in Gujarat effected by its senior leader Shankarsinh Vaghela that saw the saffron party losing power, Modi was moved to Delhi in 1995 and was made the national secretary of the party in-charge of five major states.

Modi, however, was sent back to Gujarat by BJP when the state was despondent after the massive quake and the then Chief Minister Keshubhai Patel faced criticism from many quarters for his government's performance.

As he assumed Chief Ministership replacing Patel on October 6, 2001, Modi had little idea that he was set to play long inninigs at the helm of affairs in the state.

He had said that he had come to play a "one day match" in Gujarat. But the attack on Sabarmati Express on February 27, 2002 and the subsequent communal riots changed everything and ensured he became the longest-serving Chief Minister of Gujarat.

Despite coming under fire from almost all quarters for handling of post-Godhra riots, Modi used it to his electoral advantage by taking out `Gaurav Yatra' and helping BJP to post a landslide victory in state assembly elections held in December 2002.

Modi was sworn in as the Chief minister for the second term on December 22, 2002 after which he tried to do a make-over to his "Hindutva" image by projecting himself as a development-oriented person.

His last five-year tenure will largely be remembered for his attempt to attract industries and investments into Gujarat by organising investment summits under the banner of "Vibrant Gujarat".

Apart from trying to make Gujarat a favourite investment destination, Modi also tried to woo tourists by popularising local festivals of Navratri and Uttarayan (Kite).

He also took the intiative to raise the controversial Narmada Dam's height above 100 meters. Though criticised by environment activists, Modi went on to raise the dam's height to 121 meters.

Though large sections of farmers and other communities were unhappy with his policies, industries thrived during his regime and the condition of the infrastructure in the state improved.

Modi's style of functioning earned him several critics within BJP and he had to grapple with revolt to his leadership with the rebels rallying around Keshbubhai Patel, Suresh Mehta and Kanshiram Rana.

However, Modi consolidated the grip over the party's state unit by building his own followers, purging some of his opponents by having the party take disciplinary action against them .

There were certain established norms in Indian politics till Prime Minister Narendra Modi burst onto the national scene. It was expected that Hindus would largely vote on caste lines and minorities would exercise their franchise in a bloc. This created hurdles for a party like the Bharatiya Janata Party which largely fought elections on a Hindutva plank, with a North Indian appeal base, and prevented it from coming to power at the Centre with a majority.

Before the BJP came to power in 2014, and returned stronger in 2019, ending decades of coalition politics, parties like the Congress or socialist parties banding together, covering a 'big tent' of competing and complimentary interests of various regional, tribal and religious communities, usually got a majority.

The year 2014, and more so 2019, changed all that, with the BJP being able to appeal to a large section of society (a vocal minority still opposed it). Confirmed support bases of opposition parties could not stand up to the BJP's onslaught, and the party registered victories in States like Manipur, Assam, and the rest of the Northeast, formed a government in Jammu and Kashmir, and also won Lok Sabha seats in

Telangana.

IV
Expansion Of Bjp

The expansion of the BJP began with the emergence of **Narendra Modi** on the political centrestage. The party had declared Modi its prime ministerial candidate for the 2014 general elections. In the next few years, the party continued its winning streak in state after state at the cost of the Congress party.

In the 2019 general election, the BJP clinched a second consecutive majority in the Lok Sabha, an achievement last secured by the Congress Party in 1980 and 1984. This time the BJP alone won 303 of the 543 seats, while the NDA as a whole bagged 353 seats in a landslide victory. The Congress won 52 seats, just eight more than its 2014 tally.

Eight years since the elevation of Narendra Modi, the BJP, with its allies, has methodically expanded its footprint across the states. Before the 2014 polls, the BJP was in power in just five of 29 states — lower than its previous tally of seven in 2012. Today, the BJP and its allies in the NDA govern 17 states, covering an estimated 44 per cent of the country's territory and 49.6 percent of its population.

The rise of the BJP has coincided with the marginalisation of the Congress, decimation of the Left and the decline in the strength of regional parties, though some new regional parties have come up as well. With a shrinking Congress party, Opposition to the BJP looks weak and fragmented.

"The Modi government's meteoric rise in the last eight years has brought about a paradigm shift in modern politics in India, which is today more about delivery. Indian politics is no longer just about short-term tactics and quick-fix strategies merely to win elections,

India's polarising prime minister made this an election all about himself.

He should have faced some anti-incumbency. Joblessness has risen to a record high, farm incomes have plummeted and industrial production has slumped. Many Indians were hit hard by the currency ban (also known as demonetisation), which was designed to flush out undeclared wealth, and there were complaints about what critics said was a poorly-designed and complicated uniform sales tax.

The results prove that people are not yet blaming Narendra modi for this.

On the stump, the prime minister repeatedly told people that he needed more than five years to undo more than "60 years of mismanagement". Voters agreed to give him more time.

Many Indians seem to believe that Narendra modi is a kind of messiah who will solve all their problems. A survey by the Centre for the Study of Developing Societies (CSDS), a Delhi-based think tank, a third of BJP voters said they would have supported another party if Narendra modi was not the prime ministerial candidate.

The 2014 win was partly a vote in anger against the corruption-tainted Congress party. Thursday's win is an affirmation for Narendra modi. He has become the first leader since 1971 to secure a single party majority twice in a row. "This is a victory for Modi and his vision of a new India

Aligned to this, deftly, was the promise of development. Narendra modi's targeted welfare schemes for the poor - homes, toilets, credit, cooking gas - have used technology for speedy delivery. However, the quality of these services and how much they have helped ameliorate deprivation is debatable.

Narendra modi also mined national security and foreign policy as vote-getters in a manner never seen in a general election in recent history.

After a suicide attack - claimed by Pakistan-based militants - which killed more than 40 Indian paramilitaries in disputed Kashmir and the retaliatory air strike against Pakistan in the run-up to the election, Narendra modi successfully convinced the masses that the country would be secure if he remained in power.

People having no obvious interest in foreign policy - farmers, traders, labourers - told us during our campaign travels that India had won the respect of the outside world under Narendra modi.

Narendra modi's persona has become larger than his cadre-based party, and a symbol of hope and aspiration for many.

The Bharatiya Janata Party (BJP) leader has swept to a second general election landslide. The scale of his victory stunned opponents, who'd hoped Indians wanted a change of government.

Narendra modi was propelled to power after his party's first spectacular win, in May 2014.

Since then, a lot has changed - not least the way he has promoted his brand of muscular Hindu nationalism and the manner in which he has been received as India's leader on the international stage.

It appears that Modi is slowly changing the grammar of politics. This seems to target three major classes that cut across all castes and religions: women, small and marginal farmers, and poor subalterns. From Ujjwala to Beti Bachao Beti Padhao to toilets, etc., he seems to be addressing women. Similarly, he is equally attending to the marginal farmers, putting `6,000 in their accounts annually, and giving them various other reliefs that could enhance their income. In the last eight years, the nation has not just changed under the leadership of PM Modi, but a new chapter of remarkable growth and fast-paced development is also being written.

Like in every other sphere, be it sports, business, or organisation, a good leader is the pivot around whom the entire team revolves. The leaders are the change makers. No matter how good the team is, a bad leader can lead to ruin while even a mediocre team can produce great results if it is led by a decent leader. India being a democratic country, its fate and future directly depends on the people having the option and opportunity to elect good leaders to lead it.

Sadly, while we have had politicians of every political orientation, we haven't had many good leaders. Having a good leader is the most important factor in the building of a nation

Through his mantra of 'Seva, Sushasan and Antyodaya' — service, good governance and uplifting the most marginalised — Prime Minister Narendra Modi has truly brought India to the 21st century.

In the past, the funds allocated by the central government for welfare schemes, especially grants in cash, would travel to the state governments, then to the districts, and then to the sub-divisions, development blocks, panchayats, municipalities, etc before finally reaching the beneficiary. Because there were multiple layers, it paved the way for middlemen to crop up, who demanded their 'share'. Then-Prime Minister Rajiv Gandhi had famously said that only 15 paise from every 1 rupee spent for the welfare of people reaches them.

In contrast, instead of complaining about the existing system and its inherent flaws, one of the first actions that Modi undertook as the prime minister was to change the system fundamentally and eradicate all the loopholes that made the system inefficient.

It was PM Modi's vision of Jan Dhan Yojana and demonetisation that encouraged citizens to open a bank account. This contributed immensely towards the financial inclusion of those sections who had otherwise been left out of the system. Using the JAM trinity of Jan Dhan, Aadhaar and Mobile technology, Modi transformed the way the government provided service, ensured empowerment and financial inclusion of citizens.

Initiatives like seeding of Aadhaar data with the bank accounts, Direct Benefit Transfer (DBT), development of the United Payments Interface (UPI) and the digital payments in mere eight years is nothing short of a financial miracle. The hallmark of the Modi government has been that each action was preceded by a vision, holistic planning, resource allocation, and appointment of the right agency/individual for implementation.

Today, Indians take pride in the fact that under the visionary leadership of PM Modi, there are no middlemen involved in the implementation of welfare measures. So far, almost 10,000 services of the central, state and local self-government have become available online. From scholarships, payments to farmers, government assistance, everything is transferred directly to the account of citizens.

Today, India is the world's leading nation in terms of digital economy. In 2021, 40 percent of all real-time digital financial transactions across the world originated in India, worth over Rs 20,000 crore every day, a result of PM Modi ensuring every citizen had a Jan Dhan account.

One of the key impediments towards the development of India was the lack of world-class infrastructure. Despite India achieving high growth through the decades of 1990s and early 2000s, the rate of infrastructural growth was abysmal. In 2013-14 when the UPA government was in power, only 12 km of highway was being constructed in a day, which increased to an average of 27 km per day in 2017-18.

It's the same story of growth in infrastructure be it rural roads, railways, airports, or ports. There have been various initiatives like Bharatmala, Sagarmala, inland waterways, dry/land ports, UDAN, Parvatmala, and now PM Gati Shakti, which have ensured seamless connectivity for movement of people, goods and services. Thus facilitating the last mile connectivity of infrastructure and also reducing travel time for people. All these together are set to revolutionise travel and transportation in India.

The central government under PM Modi has worked tirelessly to turn India into an international manufacturing hub. Beginning with the reduction in corporate tax rates, ensuring investment policy reforms, reduction in compliance burden to improved 'Ease of Doing Business' ranking, today India has become the leading nation to attract investment in the manufacturing sector.

Thanks to the forward thinking policies of the Modi government, today India has emerged as a leading exporter of goods and services, with total exports reaching nearly an all-time high of $670 billion in 2021-22.

This is happening because of the various programmes like Skill India, Digital India, Make in India, Vocal for Local, and performance-linked incentives among others. More importantly, all these have helped instill a sense of confidence and 'can do' attitude in Indians.

At the end of the day, there is only one measure of success when it comes to a nation — whether the measures benefit the most marginalised sections of the society.

In the last two years, the Covid-19 pandemic and the Russia-Ukraine conflict have meant that countries around the world have suffered untold miseries. Leadership remains challenged and shaken, particularly in South Asia – Sri Lanka is undergoing an economic crisis, Pakistan has seen an overturn of the government, countries like Nepal and Bangladesh are battling on the fringe of economic catastrophe, and China has locked itself down due to another surge in coronavirus cases.

Amid all this, India has emerged as the only bright spark and a ray of hope. It has administered over 192 crore vaccines as of 21 May, and supplied vaccines to numerous other countries. India has reached economic support to Nepal, Bhutan, Maldives, Bangladesh, and is rescuing Sri Lanka from its financial crisis. India has sent humanitarian aid to war-torn countries like Afghanistan and Ukraine, and is working towards finding a peaceful resolution between Russia and Ukraine.

It is to the credit of PM Modi that an International Monetary Fund paper said, "Extreme poverty was maintained below 1% in India due to Pradhan Mantri Garib Kalyan Ann Yojana."

V
most influential man in the history

Prime Minister Narendra Modi is the most influential man in the history of politicians. He has proven himself to be the man of his words, through the transformation of his revolutionary ideas into a vivid reality. It would be an understatement to call him just the 'Champion Of Development', because he also excels in every other role of an ideal Prime Minister.

1. His Stand Against Divisive Politics

Right after Modi was elected as Gujarat's Chief Minister in 2002, the Godhra riots broke out in which more than 1000 Indians were killed. It was a sensitive time which he handled well enough as a first time CM.

Since Independence there have been over 90 massacres and hundreds of riots. However, Gujarat was the only state to set up a court to investigate and jail the culprits. Modi had to face Special Investigation Team (SIT) probes several times after being alleged to have an active role, but was given the clean chit eventually.

2. His Handling Of Terrorism And Security Threats

The attacks of 26/11 proved, how vulnerable our nation was to infiltration and attacks. If it were not for NSG, Army, and police the collateral damage would have been far worse.

After the attack on Pathankot airbase every thing seemed to change, the terrorists had strict instructions from their Pakistani handlers to destroy Indian assets. The infiltration in the Pathankot airbase was detected by a drone that was deployed for regular patrolling. The authorities sealed the entire area and neutralized them in less than three days with minimal damage to civilian life and property.

Apart from this, India is also prepping its military arsenal by entering joint partnerships with France, USA, Russia and Israel. The arsenal predominantly includes nuclear capable submarines, F-16s, rockets and choppers. These will help ensure security at Indian borders at all times.

3. His Lobbying For Permanent Unsc Membership For India

Modi travelled to various countries, and was dubbed the 'NRI Prime Minister' by some. What they didn't note was that by travelling so extensively he was furthering three key agendas: improving relationships with countries, inviting investments and winning support for India's permanent seat in the United Nations Security Council (UNSC).

After travelling and inviting ambassadors and leaders from countries like the US, Germany, Russia, France and Japan, he achieved almost everyone's support for India's UNSC bid. This support was a direct result of his efforts to showcase India's eligibility for a position on this international platform.

4. Decision Making Abilities

At the time of his governance in Gujrat, PM Narendra Modi demonstrated his extraordinary decision making skills, a trait which isn't seen too often in Indian politicians. His non-nonsense approach in making key executive decisions and ensuring quick implementation are pivotal to his effective governance model.

5. Clear Vision For India's Future

PM Modi has envisioned a "long jump" for changing the economic and social face of India. Keeping the poor and underprivileged in focus of all the government policies, he has come up with P2 G2 (Pro-Poor, Proactive and Good Governance) approach.

At policy level, the Modi government will continue focusing on "Jan Dhan" or financial inclusion of the poor. The two new aspects are also included: "Jal Dhan" programmes for increasing agriculture network, and "Van Dhan" programmes for protecting forest resources.

6. Powerful Mass Appeal

Narendra Modi has a huge mass appeal and there's a strong reason as to why crowds gather in large numbers to hear him. His campaigns have been multidimensional focusing on youth empowerment, fighting corruption, wiping out terrorism and much more. With an aim to replicate socio-economic success, he strives to connect with the masses on a deeper level.

7. Contemporary Uniform Civil Code

According to Article 44 in Part IV of the Constitution of India – Directive Principles of State Policy, "The state shall endeavour to secure for the citizens a uniform civil code throughout the territory of India."

This suggests that all Indians shall be governed by common law on matters of marriage, divorce, inheritance, adoption, maintenance and the like. This puts an end to confusion and chaos of different religious personal laws and offers a fair dignity to every citizen. Modi has vowed to enforce a contemporary uniform civil code for harmonising tradition with today's times.

8. Abrogation Of Article 370

This Article comes in Part 21 of the Constitution and pertains to the Temporary, Transitional and Special Provisions. It resulted with a 1974 accord between Indira Gandhi and Sheikh Abdullah which restored peace in Jammu and Kashmir. It renders political and administrative autonomy to Jammu and Kashmir in all matters except defence, atomic energy, CBI, foreign affairs, railways, ports, maritime security, elections, currency and the like. It aimed to allow time for political injury to heal but it has turned into a bargaining tool.

For a healthy democracy, all states must be equal. Special status and special category likely create a sense of entitlement that hurts India. Either Article 370 must be removed or it must apply to all states.

9. Rationalisation Of Ministries

Modi vows to rationalise ministries and departments.It's likely that that ministries may merge to form a lean and mean cabinet. Near about 30 ministries could work more efficiently for India become more focused. The UPA had a lot of ministries which resulted in every minister doing or not doing as they pleased.

10. Proactive Diplomacy

Modi is well on his way to expand and empower India's pool of diplomats. Part of his proactive diplomacy has begun with the invites to neighbour countries for his swearing-in ceremony. It is refreshing to see New Delhi take charge. How the neighbours respond is of interest but it takes nothing away from the initiative. In time, Modi says he would work to regain the glory India once had. This is worth it. India was world mentor once and can still be so, with hard and intelligent work.

11. 100 New Cities

This ambitious plan needs vision, money, planning and brilliance. Shanghai has set a new benchmark for future cities. India's new cities ought to begin from where Shanghai left off. A key aspect should be that these cities must have aesthetic value. They ought to improve on Paris and the rest of Europe at the minimum. For this, Modi and his team would need great architects.

12. Bullet Train Quadrilateral

While world is working at their levitating train technologies, India needs its bullet trains already; the engineers speak of soil and other challenges to bullet trains in India. It sounds like alibis. A nation is stuck if its people can't travel fast. We are 50 years behind Japan on bullet trains; the world has moved on to much faster maglev trains. Five years should be the outer limit for bullet trains to start in India.

13. Infrastructure Along The LAC

India drop a few steps on the developing country ladder when it comes to infrastructure because it is either nonexistent or in a shambles. Modi has said he would lay special emphasis on developing infrastructure along the LAC at Arunachal Pradesh and Sikkim.

This means moving man and machine there and rapidly putting together super roads, bridges, communication, offices, houses and airports. China has begun work on connecting the world through high speed trains from Beijing. Surely India could at least fix its LAC act.

14. Modernise 100 Most Backward Districts

Imagine the wretched parts of India teeming with activity and progress. It would be such a boost to self-esteem and confidence. All we need is integrity, skill and speed. Hopefully, the Modi government would share a list of these 100 districts first.

15. Return Of The Kashmiri Pandits

It is a shame that our own have to be in exile in homeland. A safe and sound long-term return of the Kashmiri Pandits could help heal in a big way. It ought to be the first of many such correctives going all the way to the Maoists in Chhattisgarh.

16. Back To Basics

The Swacch Bharat Abhiyan is a wonderful example of how the PM has managed to reign in the children and the youth of the country to battle the issue of cleanliness and hygiene – a traditional concern of India. In the process, he has managed to introduce healthy competition by naming clean cities and clean railway stations as well, putting cleanliness on the national agenda.

17. Economic Leadership

The NaMo government's focus on the economic development of the country is undeniable. It is here that we should let numbers do the talking. In economic growth rate of the country in 2013-14 was pegged at about 4.7 percent, a slight increase over the 4.5 percent growth of 2012-13.

Compare this with the GDP growth of 7.6 percent as reported for 2015-16. The average inflation of India in 2013 was estimated at 10.92 percent and in 2016 it was estimated at about 6.00 percent.

18. Empowering India

"Make in India" These three words declared by the PM from the ramparts of the Red Fort woke the nation up to its potential. For years, India has been grappling with the menace of unemployment but the PM's vision to transform India into the manufacturing hub of the world has breathed new life into about 25 different sectors. Foreign investment is pouring in with Ease of Doing Business rankings climbing steadily. Add to this Modi's flagship campaigns – Skills India and Digital India and the nation is turning into one of the best startup incubation centers in the world.

19. Leading The World

India has been quite a docile follower despite its immense capabilities. Under PM Narendra Modi India seems to have broken out of its shell. Be it with regard to the BRICS bank or the PM MOdi, along with French President François Hollande, launched an alliance of over 120 nations – the Solar Alliance – at Paris COP21 climate summit. He volunteered to set up the headquarters in Gurgaon, India, once again bringing our nation to the forefront. Under NaMo, India has emerged from the shadows and taken on the lead in the global space.

20. One Nation One Market

It's been 70 years since our independence and Sardar Patel united different provinces to form a united India. The political union did turn into a reality for India but it didn't become one market. PM Modi-led Government aims to unite Indian markets to empower our producers & strengthen our consumers. With this vision, the NDA government has taken numerous initiatives to really achieve One Nation, One Market.

21. Empowering Farmers For A Prosperous India

PM Modi-led government has laid unprecedented focus on agriculture. Several initiatives have been taken for improving productivity, safeguarding farmers and augmenting their incomes and improving their overall well-being. These significant steps of the government are helping farmers in many ways including easy availability of fertilizers, improving irrigation facilities, easy access to credit, scientific help and better price for their produce. PM Modi also aims to double farmers' incomes by 2022 through multi-modal interventions.

22. *Swachh Bharat Mission*

While launching the Swachh Bharat Mission at Rajpath, New Delhi in 2014, PM Narendra Modi had said, "A clean India would be the best tribute India could pay to Mahatma Gandhi on his 150 birth anniversary in 2019." While spearheading the nationwide movement for cleanliness, PM Modi urged people to fulfil Mahatma Gandhi's dream of a clean India. As a result of that, this campaign became successful.

23. *Jan Dhan – Financial Inclusion*

When the Narendra Modi led government came into power in May 2014, millions of people in India didn't have a bank account. Several decades had passed but financial inclusion remained far-fetched to millions of Indians. So to ensure financial inclusion to one and all, the Jan Dhan Yojana was launched as a mission.

As a result, 23.93 crore bank accounts have been opened within 2 years' span. Moreover, Rs. 41,789 crore have been deposited in these bank accounts. This will help in securing future and bringing stability to lives of millions of people with the savings they will have in their bank accounts. It has also opened doors to institutional credit who were until now affected by lenders and their high interest rates. The Jan Dhan Bank account also comes with overdraft, insurance, that are now being used widely.

24. *Beti Bachao, Beti Padhao*

PM Modi launched Beti Bachao Beti Padhao on 22 January, 2015 at Panipat, Haryana. This mission was initiated to address the worsening Child Sex Ratio (CSR) and issues related to women empowerment over a life-cycle. It is an effort of three ministries: Ministries of Women and Child Development, Health & Family Welfare and Human Resource Development.

The major elements of the scheme are Enforcement of PC & PNDT Act, nation-wide awareness and advocacy campaign and multi-sectoral action in the 100 chosen districts that are low on CSR. A strong emphasis has been laid on the change of mindset through training, sensitization, awareness raising and community mobilization on ground.

25. *Saansad Adarsh Gram Yojana*

On 11 October 2014, Saansad Adarsh Gram Yojana was launched with an aim of translating the radical vision of Mahatma Gandhi about making an ideal Indian village a reality. Under this initiative, every Member of Parliament needs to adopt a Gram Panchayat and usher its overall progress thereby considering social development more important than the infrastructure. The 'Adarsh Grams' will turn into schools of local development and governance and will thus inspire other Gram Panchayats.

By taking villagers into account and using scientific tools to utmost advantage, a Village Development Plan is drafted under the Member of Parliament's leadership. After that, departments prepare detailed project reports and submit to the state government. State Level Empowered Committee (SLEC) reviews, suggests amendments and renders priority allocation of resources. As of now, several Ministries /Departments of Government of India have amended 21 Schemes in order to prioritize the SAGY Gram Panchayat projects.

26. Unleashing India's Entrepreneurial Energy

PM Modi's government has taken major steps to give a boost to entrepreneurship. The 'Make In India' initiative focuses on not only manufacturing sectors but services and infrastructure sectors as well. A 3 pronged strategy adopted by government is based on 3 C Model to work upon Compliances, Capital & Contract Enforcement.

27. Powering India's Growth

India is on an ambitious mission to provide electricity to 18,000 villages that continue to fraught with darkness after almost 7 decades of independence. PM Modi had announced on 15 August 2017 that all the remaining villages will be electrified within 1000 days.

Rural electrification is taking place rapidly and is being done in a truly transparent way. It is worth noting that the electricity reaching the villages is accompanied by dreams, aspirations & upward mobility in life for villagers.

28. Ganga Rejuvenation Project- Namami Gange

The River Ganga supports more than 600 million people, that's about 40% of India's population. In order to turn this vision into reality, the Government launched an integrated Ganga conservation mission called 'Namami Gange' to curb the ever-increasing pollution of Ganga River and revive the river. The Union Cabinet sanctioned the action plan that was proposed by Centre regarding spending Rs 20,000 crores till 2019-2020 on cleaning the river and increasing the budget by four times and with 100% central share – a central sector scheme.

29. *Make In India*

'Make in India' is a revolutionary initiative launched by PM Narendra Modi to give an impetus to entrepreneurship. Its four pillars are: new processes to promote 'ease of doing business', new and modern infrastructure for industries' growth, new sectors (25 sectors have been identified in all the sectors) and new mindset of being a facilitator rather than a regulator.

30. *Unprecedented Transparency*

In the past decades, we have witnessed arbitrary decision making, corruption and discretion rather than policy dictating crucial decisions. After Supreme Court's decision of cancelling the coal block allocations, the current government took swift action to ensure transparent and timely auctions. The Auction and Allotment revenue from 67 coal blocks have reached 3.35 lakh crores over the life of the mine.

The long-time pending defence band identification was resolved swiftly and good quantity of 2100 MHz released by the Defence Ministry was put into the auction. Various rounds of auction were carried out for spectrum in 4 different bands: 800 MHz, 900 MHz, 1800 MHz and 2100 MHz. The approved reserve price was Rs 80277 crore but the auction ended up fetching a record of Rs.109875 crore. Apart from this, Environment Ministry began process of online submission of applications to ensure online tracking and facilitate informed, transparent, expeditious and predictable decisions on forest approval applications.

Moreover, the government is working in tandem with Swiss Government and procuring case details investigated by IT

Department. The Government sanctioned the Undisclosed Foreign Income and Assets (Imposition of Tax) Bill 2015. The Provisions of the Bill include severe penalties and punishment for undisclosed foreign income and assets. It is also mandatory to quote PAN for purchase or sale of above Rs. 1 lakh.

31. Connecting India like Never Before

PM Modi's government has been giving a huge boost to infrastructure. Railways, Roads, and Shipping have been the focus to augment this infrastructure and aid in connectivity. The Railway budget focuses on structural and infrastructural reforms.New trains are announced on a regular rather than annual basis.

Various passenger-friendly amenities including Wi-fi on railway stations, passenger helpline (138), security helpline (182), paperless unreserved ticketing, e-catering, mobile security app and CCTV cameras for safety of women, etc have been launched. The railways will serve as a locomotive of the economy and connect mines, coasts, etc.

32. Empowering Different States Equally With Boost To Federalism

PM Modi has stressed on the need to leverage co-operative & competitive federalism to achieve all round growth. For a long time, we have seen a Big Brother relationship between the Centre & States. A 'One Size Fits All' approach had been used for years, not taking into account the heterogeneity of different states and their local requirements.

The NITI Aayog was formed to further empower and

strengthen the states. An important evolutionary change from the past will be replacing a Union-to-State one-way flow of policy by a genuine and continuing partnership with the states. NITI Aayog will act with speed, to provide the strategic policy vision for the government as well as deal with contingent issues.

33. *Putting The Indian Economy On A Fast-Track*

India's GDP Growth rocketed to 7.4%, which is the fastest among all the large economies of the world. Various rating agencies and think tanks have predicted that India's growth would accelerate sharply in the next few years under the NDA Government. Banking on the strong fundamentals & reforms being undertaken by the NDA Government, Moody's upgraded India's rating from 'stable' to 'positive' recently.

When BRICS was launched, a lot of people felt that the "I" (India) does not belong to the league and India was seen with skepticism. Now, it is India which is perceived to be powering the BRICS as its growth engine.

34. *Smart Cities Mission*

Smart Cities Mission is an urban renewal and retrofitting program by the Government of India with a mission to develop 100 cities all over the country making them citizen friendly and sustainable. The Union Ministry of Urban Development is responsible for implementing the mission in collaboration with the state governments of the respective cities.

35. *The World Does Yoga Together*

International Yoga Day is celebrated annually on 21 June since its inception in 2015. An international day for yoga was declared unanimously by the United Nations General Assembly (UNGA). Yoga is a physical, mental and spiritual practice attributed mostly to India. The Indian Prime Minister Narendra Modi in his UN address suggested the date of 21 June, as it is the longest day of the year in the Northern Hemisphere and shares special significance in many parts of the world.

36. In humanity We Trust

When the conflict in Yemen reached its peak there were people of several nations stuck on the conflict zone. The Government of India left no stone unturned to rescue people, not only Indian but of several Nations. Several Nations sought India's assistance in rescue operations and the scale and speed at which India's rescue operations was unprecedented and highly impactful.

37. Goods And Services Tax (GST)

Earlier, because of multiple tax structures, maximum resources of transport and logistics sector were expended in maintaining paperwork. The Pollution levels have also come down with the increased speeds of the trucks. Goods are also being transported much faster. The time required to cover distances has come down drastically. Highways have become clutter-free.

38. One Rank, One Pension

The implementation of OROP resulted in enhanced pension for the pensioners/family pensioners of Defence Forces. The setting up of the Judicial Committee headed by Justice L. Narasimha Reddy did help in the removal of anomalies that may arise in the implementation of OROP.

39. StartUp India

Start-ups are now exempted from paying income tax on their profit for the first three years. The Government has introduced a simple exit policy for Start-ups along with a scheme of fast-tracking of Start-up patent applications.

Eighty percent exemption in patent fee for Start-up businesses, and a self-certification based compliance system for Start-ups would be introduced for 9 labour and environment laws. The Atal Innovation Mission was also launched to give a boost to innovation.

40. No Doubt A Bold Step Demonetization

Demonetization of currency means discontinuity of the said currency from circulation and replacing it with a new currency.

Most of the people hailed the Modi's strong decision, while poor were shocked by the move. The overnight decision changed the life of many as black money holders were worried about the pile of cash they were sitting on. Many poor daily wage workers were left with no job and income as owners were unable to pay their daily wage.

41. He believes in Teamwork

PM Modi seems to attribute every bit of success to the party and their team work in the hour of need. Modi can be seen diverting all the credits coming his way to his dedicated team. "Teamwork is the essence of good governance. It is necessary to form a team within the party and also within the administrative system."

42. E-governance is easy, effective and economical

E-governance has been strongly backed by PM Narendra Modi for not only being easy, effective and economical but also because it is environment-friendly and will result in paperless offices. Technology, indeed, has the power to transform our economic potential. Bridging the digital divide, IT acts as an enabler for change.

National eGovernance Plan (NeGP) has been formulated with an aim to improve delivery of government services to citizens and businesses. The major activities include setting up ICT infrastructure, implementation of national and state level e-governance projects, R&D etc.

43. Information Technology + Indian Talent = India Tomorrow

According to PM Narendra Modi, embracing technology cannot happen if only a few people are keen on it and the scale has to be larger. Technology has power to transform our economic potential also. IT + IT = IT. This means 'Information technology + Indian Talent = India Tomorrow'.

44. Respecting the dignity of women

Out of over 24 crore households in India, India about 10 crore households are deprived of LPG as cooking fuel and use primary cooking sources such as firewood, coal and dung cakes. The smoke produced by burning these fuels badly affects the women and children's health and causes various respiratory disorders.

Since the launch of Pradhan Mantri Ujjwala Yojana in May

2016, the food fuel and housing inflation has almost halved from 6.44% in May'16 to 3.05% in October'17. This initiative aims to empower poor women who inhale unhealthy emissions from burning coal, wood and other such cooking fuels. Over 3 crore LPG connections have been released across India until now.

45. Stand-Up India

PM Narendra Modi launched 'Stand up India' on 5 April 2016 to back women entrepreneurs and SC/ST communities in non-farm sector. This scheme offers bank loans of 10 lakh-1 crore repayable upto 7 years. It provides handholding support at both pre-loan stage and during operations such as registration with online platforms and e-marketplaces and sessions on best practices.

46. He Interacts with People through his official app & Social Media

Our Prime Minister Narendra Modi is digital savvy and is very active on social media. In a first, the official app of PM Modi provides latest information, instant updates and allows people of India to contribute toward several tasks. By sharing ideas and suggestions, people of India get an exclusive opportunity to receive emails and messages directly from the PM. It has some features that empower citizens to make a positive difference in the society. On its thoughtful forums, one can share ideas, views and interact with a wide range of people.

47. His Numerous Measures To Attract Foreign Direct Investment (FDI) to India

In three years of Modi's governance, the inflow of FDI has considerably gone up by 38%, from $36 billion in

2013-14 to $60 billion in 2016-17. Bold policy reforms and 'Make in India' initiative have especially played a major role in driving FDI to India. It was even regarded as the "topmost attractive destination for foreign investment" according to a release.

48. Expand scope of Food Security Act

When National Food Security Act was rolled out by 33 states/UTs in 2016, the Centre extended its scope by making foodgrain available to India's 12 crore "poorest of poor" for free. The poorest 2.5 crore households now get 35 kg each of highly subsidised foodgrain (rice, wheat and coarse cereals) a month under the Antoydaya Anna Yojana (AAY).

49. Give Up LPG Subsidy

"Give it up" campaign urged well-off sections of society to forgo LPG subsidy so that it can be utilized in giving subsidized LPG connections to the poor. This would help BPL house ladies get kitchen comfort by reducing carbon emissions due to firewood burning.

50. Saubhagya on electrification

Pradhan Mantri Sahaj Bijli Har Ghar Yojana is a scheme that aims to provide electricity connections to more than 40 million households in rural and urban areas.

51. Securing our nation, Restoring its pride

Our Indian Army has been tough against terror and gave a strong fightback to the enemy by doing surgical strike in which it destroyed terrorist launchpads in 2016. This bold move was also backed globally. Moreover, it carried out an operation to eliminate a group of insurgents in Myanmar.

52. *His reforms led to Moody's upgrading India's rating for first time in 14 years*

It's the result of structural reforms undertaken by Modi government that the international rating agency Moody's Investors Service upgraded India's sovereign rating for the first time in 14 years.

53. *The Indigenous financial engine Mudra Bank*

In Pradhan Mantri Mudra Yojana, the companies which needing funds less than Rs. 10 lacs can easily apply for loan under this scheme. It is highly beneficial for small business, non-farm sector businesses and non-corporates. In this scheme, age for filing loan is 23-28 years and the loan should be paid back before reaching 65 years' age.

54. *Eco-Friendly steps taken by Modi*

Under Modi government, various steps have been taken toward achieving eco-friendly goals for a sustainable future. The widely successful campaign Swachh Bharat Abhiyan, Clean Ganga Mission, National Air Quality Index, Toilets Before Temples, and Clean Mission for Mount Everest.

55. *Modi represents New India*

Marking 70 years of India's independence, Prime Minister Narendra Modi urged people and outlining the vision of 'Unify India' (Bharat Jodo) in which he aims to build a "New India" that will be free of caste and religious differences, corruption and terrorism and where all the Indians will get access to housing, electricity and water.

56. *India becoming a hub of quality education*

PM Modi has also set out to bring structural reforms in school and university education. The functioning of Niti Ayog that focuses on government's mission of 'grade-wise learning for each class', the University Grants Commission and restructuring All India Council of Technical Education (AICTE) has been emphasized.

57. Women & Child Development

PM Modi has taken serious initiatives to provide aid to pregnant and lactating mothers for a comfortable birth. Pradhan Mantri Matritva Vandana Yojana provides Rs. 6000 of financial aid to pregnant mothers on their first live birth. Moreover, another scheme named Pradhan Mantri Surakshit Matritv Abhiyan aims to offer assured, comprehensive and quality antenatal care services to all pregnant women on 9th of every month for free.

58. Special gift for Meritorious Muslim girls

Modi government encouraged Muslim girls to pursue higher education and those obtaining graduate degrees and have got MAEF scholarships earlier will get Rs. 15,00 as a wedding gift. This scheme has been called Shaadi Shagun.

59. He works really hard

PM Modi's dream for new, better India is so vivid and his love for country is so selfless that he doesn't even need Sundays off and some sources even say that he works tirelessly for 20 hours a day and sleeps only for about 3-4 hours.

60. India can defend itself in times of terror

Bold steps taken against terrorism by Modi government include carrying out surgical strikes across the Line of

Control (LoC) in Kashmir, resuming cordon and search operations in more than 20 villages in Shopian and combing operations launched against Maoists in Chhattisgarh among many others.

61. Mera Aadhaar Meri Pehchan

Aadhar card serves as a proof of one's identity and address anywhere in India. It helps in instantly opening bank account and obtaining monthly pension, passport in 10 days, PF money and student scholarship.

62. Green Energy has got a boost under Modi regime

Modi to raise solar investment target to $100 Billion by 2022. The investments will help boost the alternative energy capacity to 100,000 MW. The Government wants to raise renewable capacity to 175 gigawatts by 2022 from 45 gigawatts at present. The impact can already be seen with the public commute vehicles switching to electric and other renewable energy sources.

Government also issued Rs 42,000 crore for afforestation with Parliament passing The Compensatory Afforestation Fund Bill, 2016.

63. Empowering Indians

Prime Minister Narendra Modi has lived up to his mantra of "sabka saath sabka vikas" (development for all) by empowering Indians not just in the country but also those living abroad. In the last three years, the government had managed to evacuate 1.25 lakh people from troubled places in different parts of the world

64. Initiative For Women Empowerment Revolution in India

Out of the several schemes that the modi government launched these are a few which falls under the category of Women Empowerment:

Beti Bachao Beti Padhao

The One Stop Centre

Women Helpline

Nari Shakti Puraskar

And there were few amendments in the existing women empowerment schemes too.

65. Housing For All

Prime Minister Narendra Modi's flagship housing scheme 'Pradhan Mantri Gramin Awas Yojna' came with the aim of providing 'Housing For All' by 2022. The credit linked subsidy scheme (CLSS) on home loans under the Pradhan Mantri Awas Yojana has now been extended till March 2019.

66. No place for VIP culture in New India

Soon after the Union Cabinet decided to ban red beacons on VIP cars, Prime Minister Narendra Modi said people must also move away from the mindset of VIP culture. Stressing that if every person is considered important in a country of 1.25 billion people, he said India can achieve great things.

67. First leader in India to connect with people through radio

In fifteen addresses of Mann ki Baat broadcast so far, more than 61,000 ideas have been received on the website and 1.43 lakh audio recordings by listeners have been received. Each month, some selected calls become a part of the broadcast. 02 June 2017, PM Narendra Modi's 'Mann Ki Baat' was also available in regional dialects, starting with Chhattisgarh, Haryana and Jharkhand.

68. *His Moral values towards Nation*

One can say that PM Modi does what he preaches, and it is a sign of a man who is still in touch with his roots; a man who wants to advance but not at the cost of his cultural values. For PM Modi the nation comes first, maybe that's one of the reason why he works 18 hours a day. (Narendra Modi believes in India, Indian values, and it's traditions. Hence he insists his colleagues and officials to go in for Indian dresses when bonus official duties.

Narendra Modi has maintained high moral ground. Also he is a very hard working one, putting in 18 hours a day work. Modi doesn't waste his time. Hence when on tour, he travels during night and keeps the day time for official work. For Modi nation comes first. Hence many decisions, even if they affect the party electorally, implements them. Narendra Modi appreciates and encourages any one who does good work even if he is from opposition.

Modi do not considers his adversaries within the party or outside, as his enemies. If they are merited he takes them into the cabinet as in the case of Sushma Swaraj. He congratulated Nitish Kumar on his victory though he was his adversary.

69. *He is Man of Rule*

At Times Modi has Addressed the BJP Parliamentary meeting, saying that he was disappointed with the attendance percentage of BJP MPs and that there is an urgent need to overcome the flaw. Proving that he is a man of rule and he is willing to tie all the loose ends in order to establish order.

70. Growth in Agriculture

To resolve the problem of unpredictable nature of farming and prevent farmer suicides in the country, the Government launched PM Mantri Fasal Bima Yojana in early 2016. It's a crop insurance policy with relaxed premium rates on the principal sum insured for farmers. Implemented with a budget of Rs 17,600 crore, this scheme will provide financial support to farmers and cover for their losses.

71. What Makes Narendra Modi Different?

Modi is a leader who has both power and passion. We have seen political leaders who had visionary thinking and we have seen some leaders who had an eye for the details, but Narendra Modi can do both. While his eyes are focused on the stars his feet are firmly on the ground.

72. Your bank account is now key to security as well

Pradhan Mantri Suraksha Bima Yojana is available to people between 18 and 70 years of age with bank accounts. It has an annual premium of ₹12 exclusive of taxes. The GST is exempted on Pradhan Mantri Suraksha Bima Yojana. The amount will be automatically debited from the account. The accident insurance scheme will have one year cover from June 1 to May 31 and would be offered through banks and administered through public sector general insurance companies.

73. *Har Ghar Bijli...Har Ghar Paani...Gaon Gaon Faili Khushaali...*

The DDUGJY scheme will enable to initiate much awaited reforms in the rural areas. It focuses on feeder separation (rural households & agricultural) and strengthening of sub-transmission & distribution infrastructure including metering at all levels in rural areas. This will help in providing round the clock power to rural households and adequate power to agricultural consumers .

74. *Disclose Your Undisclosed Income to Transform India*

The government had launched PMGKY after the demonetisation of high value currency as a second chance for tax evaders to come clean.

Under the scheme, holders of black money in the demonetised currency notes could declare the undisclosed income and pay penalty and tax of up to 50 per cent of the funds and park 25 per cent in non-interest bearing deposit for four years.

75. *Driving India towards a cashless driven country*

PM Modi has been giving a big push towards making India a digitally empowered and cashless economy. Bharat Interface for Money (BHIM) aims to empower poor, dalits, tribals and farmers by using secure fingerprint access system for making transactions. Internet banking, mobile banking, Aadhaar Enabled Payment System (AEPS) are other digital payment methods.

76. *Make a contribution in honour of the Bravehearts*

'Bharat Ke Veer' is an initiative calling out to civilians to contribute to the families of martyred soldiers. The portal allows general public to donate money online directly to individual braveheart's account and or Bharat Ke Veer's corpus.

77. Quality medicines at affordable prices for all

Quality branded medicines are not affordable to all so Pradhan Mantri Jan Aushadhi Pariyojana Kendra was launched to provide quality generic medicines at affordable prices to the masses through special kendras.

78. Rejuvenating the soul of Urban India

India is a country with rich heritage and culture. This scheme aims to preserve and revitalize the heritage city's soul so as to reflect the city's unique ethos by fostering accessible, informative and secured environment.

This scheme is being implemented in 12 cities namely, Ajmer, Amaravati, Amritsar, Badami, Dwarka, Gaya, Kanchipuram, Mathura, Puri, Varanasi, Velankanni and Warangal.

79. His revolutionary initiative for water conservation

To address the ever-growing water crisis in the country, Jal Kranti Abhiyan was launched in June 2015 to preserve the precious water. It would involve using modern technique for enhancing water security, encouraging combined use of surface and groundwater, creating additional facilities for water conservation through construction of water harvesting structures, widespread programme for rain-water harvesting and for motivating the villagers toward participation in the water related schemes and cost-sharing by the community to promote a sense of belongingness and accountability.

80. *SANKALP SE SIDDHI (New India Movement 2017-2022)*

Sankalp Se Siddhi scheme is a 5-year plan of building new India by focusing on major issues such as Corruption-free, Literate India, Poverty-free, Communalism free, Caste discrimination free, Clean India and Terrorism Free. It also aims to double low income group families especially poor farmers' income.

81. *Growing international tourist arrivals*

Modi's tourism push has truly paid off. International tourist arrivals (ITAs) has seen a significant jump of 16 places within past 2 years according United Nations World Tourism Organisation's World Tourism Barometer. In 2015, India was at 40th place and it recorded 24th place this March 2017. Pilgrimage Rejuvenation and Spiritual Augmentation Drive (PRASAD) scheme was launched to develop and beautify of pilgrimage sites to drive growth of domestic tourists. Moreover, 27 projects of Rs. 2261 crore have been sanctioned for 21 states and UTs.

82. *Healthcare Initiatives*

In the healthcare sector, several initiatives have been taken to free India from issue of open defecation to prevent diseases including typhoid, cholera, hepatitis among others. Sikkim, Himachal Pradesh and Kerala have recently been declared as first three open defecation-free states. Clean India Initiative (Swachh Bharat mission), E-health, door-to-door screening of various chronic diseases are few other initiatives taken by Modi government. The launch of

New Health Policy seeks to to escalate public health facilities by 50% by 2025.

83. Secularism: India First

Modi's stand for secularism can be seen in his speeches and in his actions too. Secularism is a term interpreted in many different ways by different people. PM Modi mantra is made quite clear with this statement of his "For me, it has always been something very simple - putting India First." The OFBJP(Overseas Friends Of Bhartiya Janta Party), a BJP sympathiser group has presence across 12 states in the US. The body claims to work towards projecting a positive and correct image of India and its people in the US and foreign media.

84. ISRO Makes History

ISRO and Department of Science successfully accomplished 36 missions in the last three years. Which includes 17 launch vehicle missions, 16 satellites mission and 3 technology demonstration missions. Most notable feat was that the ISRO launched a record 104 satellites in one go using PSLV. Government also made huge investments in an effort of preparedness for disaster management with Monitoring of drought, floods, and cyclones are being done.

85. Modi's India Is Rising

According to a Forbes article Modi has done well in his term of just 3 years in comparison to the long reigning former government.India's rise in the last couple of years is evident in international rankings. Like the World Bank's 2017 ranking of "ease of doing business," from 130 last year to 100 this year. And the World Economic Forum Report

(WEFR) competitiveness ranking, which ranked India 40th out of 137 countries included in the report, the highest it has ever been, up from 71st three years ago.

86. Fearless Leader

According to John Chambers, the executive head of Cisco Systems and the chairman of newly constituted US-India Strategic Partnership Forum (USISPF); Prime Minister Narendra Modi is a 'fearless' leader who would tirelessly pursue the path of economic reform,

87. 3rd most trusted Govt in the world

India securing third best place in the list of most trusted governments worldwide is an evidence that the country is treading in the right direction of development under our Honorable PM Modi's leadership. The report reveals that almost three quarters (74 percent) of Indians say they have confidence in their national government.The factors taken into consideration were- the economy, political upheaval, and headline-grabbing events like major corruption cases.

88. Modi and his "Yaari Dosti"

PM Narendra Modi has been in talks for long because of his frequent foreign visits. The countries that he visited in an effort to improve the friendly ties between India and the world are Russia Balochistan Pakistan Britain Australia and The United States Of America. People have been giving him names like NRI PM and what not.
Modi's foreign visits, however, have certainly placed India in a strong strategic position internationally.

89. He Is Among World's 10 Most Powerful People

Prime Minister Narendra Modi has been ranked among the top 10 most powerful people in the world by Forbes in a list that has been topped by Russian President Vladimir Putin for a fourth straight year and had US President-elect Donald Trump in the second place.

90. Law & Order

With the Narendra Modi government celebrating the completion of three years in power at the Centre, the Ministry of Law and Justice has highlighted its 40 achievements, including the appointment of 17 judges to the Supreme Court and 232 judges to various high courts since May 2014.

91. Not A Single Corruption Charge Against Modi Govt

PM Modi projected his government's success in the areas of fighting terror and graft, Prime Minister Narendra Modi has said that there has not been a single stain of corruption against his regime and no country has questioned the surgical strikes conducted across the border.

92. Revolution in the Air

UDAN-RCS, UDAN (Ude Desh ka Aam Naagrik) is a regional airport development and "Regional Connectivity Scheme" (RCS) of Government of India, with the objective of "Let the common citizen of the country fly", aimed at making air travel affordable and widespread, to boost inclusive national economic development, job growth and air transport infrastructure development of all regions and states of India.

93. Shramev Jayate

To usher in labor reforms, Shramev Jayate scheme was launched in 2014. The wage ceiling of laborers was raised Rs 6500 per month to Rs 15000 per month all throughout the country. It even aims to improve employability through skill development programmes for laborers by promoting the Industrial Training Institutes.

94. Infrastructure Initiatives

Multiple infrastructure projects have been launched and some are on the brink of implementation. Rs. 12,00,000 crore Sagarmala project of building more than 6 mega ports, Rs 50,800-crore Setu Bharatam project of renovating 1500 British era bridges, Rs 1198 crore project of building world's highest bridge on Chenab and several others are key projects initiated under Modi government.

95. Promises that were never kept are now being taken care of

Even after more than 65 years of independence, "Garibi Hatao" has been an age-long slogan being given by politicians in every election. But the fact is that any serious initiative to solve such a huge problem have hardly been taken. And Modi government and has truly transformed the lives of many through its numerous initiatives.

96. Ek Bharat Shreshtha Bharat

India is a country celebrating the spirit of 'unity in diversity'. Its diverse cultures, languages and traditions has led to the Ek Bharat Shreshtha Bharat programme that aims to enhance interaction across varied geographies, ensuring the geopolitical strength and building learning ecosystem through State to State connect.

97. Solving Long Pending Issues

Modi government has played a key role in solving several long-time pending issues. Now, there's no more free reign for black money, no more worries on OROP (One Rank One Position), no more villages in dark and land boundary agreement with Bangladesh has been implemented.

98. Prakash Path – Way to Light

Conserving power is much more economical than producing power. So PM Modi launched scheme for energy conservation by promoting use of LED bulbs for home and street lighting.

99. Initiative to bring students closer to nature

To bring school students closer to natural environment, School Nursery Yojana was launched in 2015 to raise plant nurseries. This will help them in understanding the natural processes of germination and feel the joy of watching sapling grow.

100. Conserve and develop indigenous bovine breeds

Enhancing the productivity of indigenous breeds of India through professional farm management and superior nutrition is the major idea behind Rashtriya Gokul Mission for Farmers. Rs 150 crore has been sanctioned for the project.

101. Skill Development and Entrepreneurship

The National Apprenticeship Promotion Scheme aims to provide apprenticeship training to over 50 lakh youngsters in order to create more jobs. It has budgetary outlay of Rs 10000 crore. NAPS is implemented by Director General of

Training (DGT) under the aegis of Union Ministry of Skill Development and Entrepreneurship (MSDE).

102. Follower of Swami Vivekananda

Narendra Modi is a follower of Swami Vivekananda which shows in his shared ideologies with Swami Vivekananda who had given the concept of 'One Asia.' He said that the solutions to the world's problems will come from Asia. Today, the world says 21st century is Asia's century.

One Asia has the potential to solve the world's problems. We should look at his ideas in today's concept.

Modi's election to the Centre was particularly significant, given that it was for the first time in 3 decades that a single party won the majority seats to form the government at the Centre. BJP racked up a stunning 282 seats on its own, the highest number of seats won by any party on its own since the 1984 Lok Sabha elections when the Congress, led by then prime minister Rajiv Gandhi won a decisive victory.

Modi's triumph was also considered momentous, for it came against the backdrop of myriad corruption scams, failure of the nation's foreign policy, chronic economic distress and a general sense of policy paralysis at the centre. The Manmohan Singh-led UPA government had failed on multiple fronts, sparking anger among the citizens for squandering a crucial opportunity accorded to them to transform the country and usher it into an era of prosperity.

However, as the emergence of corruption scams one after the other became the highlight of the second tenure of the UPA government, the public disillusionment with the Centre, coupled with PM Modi's impressive record in leading Gujarat, catapulted voters to the BJP, propelling it to the Centre once again after a decade of remaining out of power.

Then in 2019, PM Modi came back to power once again, demolishing the myth harboured by some that his election to the highest office in the land in 2014 was primarily because of the incompetence and inefficiency of the UPA government. With his victory in 2019, PM Modi proved that his government had worked for the benefit of the poor, improved India's global standing, brought prosperity to the country, restored cultural and civilisational pride and enhanced its security apparatus.

While the Modi government excelled in various fields of governance, it particularly stood out in designing and deploying a robust foreign policy that forced even bitter enemies like former Pakistan Prime Minister Imran Khan to acknowledge its merit. From shunning its "non-aligned" stance to asserting its identity on global forums to displaying zero tolerance towards terrorism emanating from its neighbouring countries to prioritising its self-interest above conformity to the western notions, India's foreign policy had undergone a remarkable transformation under the leadership of PM Modi.

However, India's foreign policy has not always been as dynamic and vibrant as it is under the Modi government. For a couple of decades after the independence, India's foreign policy was a disaster, committing one after another 'Nehruvian' blunders. For instance, not obliterating Pakistan for its audacity of attacking and capturing Jammu and Kashmir in 1948, or serving the UNSC seat to China on a platter and later on misreading China's intentions on Aksai Chin and Arunachal Pradesh that inevitably led to the catastrophic 1962 war.

But, in the last few years, after PM Modi came to power, there has been a radical shift in India's foreign policy. It carried out Surgical Strikes across the border, both in the east and west, to demonstrate its willingness to go beyond the conventional methods to deal with the scourge of terrorism. With Balakot Airstrikes, it has shown the world that it is no longer the yesteryear's India that will sit back and lick its wound, but it will mount a swift offensive and exact revenge on its adversaries.

Additionally, the foreign policy of India has also been incredibly malleable, which has helped it foreground India's interests above everything else as evident in its measured approach to dealing with the Russian invasion of Ukraine. With the Modi government completing its 8 years in office, here are some of the instances that underscore how India's foreign policy has evolved drastically under PM Modi.

India jettisons its traditionally-held non-aligned approach and displays more assertiveness in international relations

While India has traditionally been "non-aligned" in its foreign policy approach, after PM Modi came to power in 2014, New Delhi has exhibited more assertiveness in its international relations, especially in its role as an emerging superpower and its commitment toward a multi-polar rules-based global order.

By straying away from the old strategy of strict non-alignment, PM Modi has paved a way for unabashed and stronger ties with great and middle-sized powers. In doing so, PM Modi has turned India into a strategic player with a highly effective foreign policy. It has ceased to remain a bystander and has actively participated in fostering and reinforcing global alliances that have elevated its role as a country that is willing to take the leap and play an important role on the international stage.

As the world found itself in the throes of the coronavirus outbreak, India leveraged its prowess in vaccine manufacturing, developing its own vaccine in record time and rapidly scaling its capacities to manufacture vaccines developed by western organisations. As a part of its foreign diplomacy and its commitment to humanity, India exported 65 million doses of COVID-19 vaccines to more than 100 countries across the globe, which earned it the moniker of the "Pharmacy of the world."

India, under PM Modi, has also been aggressively pursuing challenges posed by Climate Change. On November 2, 2021, PM Modi pledged to cut the country's emissions to net-zero by 2070, an ambitious target for a developing country like India where fossil fuels are still the primary source of energy. PM Modi, however, has repeatedly insisted on harnessing the wellspring of renewable sources of energy available and reducing the carbon footprint of the country.

However, nothing exemplifies India's marked change in its foreign policy after 2014 than the recent picture from Tokyo that took the internet by storm. Prior to 2014, India was considered a reluctant regional power that was let down by its corrupt and byzantine governance model. But after 2014, the world has grown to admire and come to recognise the inherent potential India possessed.

In the viral image, PM Modi was seen leading a group of global leaders, including the US president Joe Biden, Australia PM Anthony Albanese and a retinue of diplomats accompanying them, underscoring the country's growing influence and stature across the world.

Zero tolerance for terrorism emanating from neighbouring countries, especially Pakistan

One of the cornerstones of the Modi government's foreign policy has been its zero tolerance for terrorism emanating from neighbouring countries, particularly Pakistan. The Indian government, under the leadership of PM Modi, has called out Pakistan's nuclear bluff on more than one occasion, sending a clear message to Islamabad and Rawalpindi, the two power centres of the dysfunctional country, that India will not be as accommodating to terror attacks as it had been during the UPA years.

While the UPA-II exhibited shocking pusillanimity in refraining from taking Pakistan to task after the dastardly Mumbai 26/11 attacks, PM Modi authorised an audacious surgical strike against the terror launchpads responsible for sending terrorists that carried out the Uri terror attack in 2016. Days after the terror attack, the Indian Armed Forces launched a counter-operation, inside Pakistan occupied Kashmir, and destroyed the terror launchpads, signalling the fundamental shift in its policy on tackling terror attacks in India, and by extension Pakistan.

Before striking along India's western borders, the Indian Armed Forces had carried out similar surgical strikes to eliminate the terrorists hiding in the thick forests of Myanmar to avenge the death of its soldiers martyred in a cowardly terror attack. Years later, in 2019, the Modi government sanctioned an unprecedented airstrike in Balakot, deep inside Pakistan, to annihilate a terror camp operated by Jaish-e-Muhammad in response to the Pulwama terror attack.

If this was not enough, the Modi government went a step ahead and abrogated the contentious Article 370 that granted Jammu and Kashmir a separate status and effected a greater integration of the state with the union of India. Two union territories—Jammu and Kashmir and Ladakh—were carved out of the erstwhile state, wresting the control of the border state from self-serving local politicians with separatist tendencies and transferring it to the Centre.

Pakistan, propagandists in India and across the world, squirmed and caterwauled over the move, but the Modi government remained steadfast on its stand that Jammu and Kashmir is an internal matter of India and those who were losing their sleep over the move had no locus standi to be bothered by the abrogation of Article 370. Pertinently, the invalidation of Article 370 struck a death blow to the terror funding in the valley, depriving the overground terror workers of the funds flowing in from across the border. As a result, incidents of stone-pelting and terror attacks came down drastically after the abrogation of Article 370.

But more importantly, the hollowing out of Article 370 demonstrated a departure from India's longstanding foreign policy on the issue of Kashmir. Past governments had extended a long rope to Pakistan and separatists in Kashmir, thereby empowering them to continue with their nefarious designs with impunity. However, with the abrogation of Article 370, in one fell swoop, India not only changed the terms of its further discussions with Pakistan but also signalled to the world that it is resolute in its commitment to bring the stolen parts of Kashmir back.

VI

Ensuring the safety of Indian expatriates in distress

For the Modi government, forging lasting relationships with foreign nations for mutual growth and development was just one facet of the foreign policy. The other important one was to ensure the safety of Indians in distress abroad. For the first few years of the first Modi government, the late Sushma Swaraj spearheaded the policy, turning Twitter into a helpline and coming to the rescue of distraught diaspora.

The Indian government has also been quite dextrous and proactive in navigating complex crises erupting in different parts of the world, effectively calibrating its response to the requirements and rescuing stranded Indians.

But executing an evacuation plan is not an easy job. It's a Herculean task, a disastrous nightmare that a country has to see through to safely rescue its people. The fluidity of the situation makes it incredibly difficult for the authorities to draw up a blueprint for the evacuation amidst perpetual volatility.

The complexity of the task at hand adds to the pressure on the government and the officials involved in the evacuation. The country is also severely constrained in case it does not share a contiguous border with the nation from where it plans to pull out its people.

Yet, the Modi government showed extraordinary gumption in evacuating people stranded in faraway places. Last year, India set in motion an evacuation plan to extract its citizens stuck in Afghanistan after the Taliban overthrew the US-backed government and took control of the country.

In 2019, India had successfully exfiltrated a CRPF contingent marooned in Libya amid a deteriorating security situation on the ground due to civil unrest. Before that, the Indian government rescued more than 4,500 Indians and 960 foreigners from war-ravaged Yemen in 2015. India also rescued 46 nurses from ISIS captivity in strife-torn Iraq in 2014.

Looking Dragon in the eye: India's uncompromising stance on protecting its territorial integrity and border security

Under the leadership of PM Modi, India has grown to assert its territorial integrity in the face of mounting Chinese aggression. While the previous governments did little to protect India's border areas from China's salami-slicing, Beijing could no longer continue its evil plans of discreetly expanding its frontiers without facing tough resistance from India.

In June 2017, Indian armed forces and China's PLA troops were engaged in a tense stand-off over the Chinese construction of a road in Doklam near a trijunction border area, known as Donglang, or Donglang Caochang. India opposed Chinese construction, expressing concern over its vicinity to the Indian border.

As a part of Operation Juniper, India deployed 270 troops armed with weapons and two bulldozers crossed the Sikkim border into Doklam to stop the Chinese troops from constructing the road. After weeks of negotiations and diplomatic manoeuvres, on 28 August 2017, both India and China announced that they had withdrawn all their troops from the face-off site in Doklam. The end of the Doklam standoff heralded possibly one of India's most spectacular diplomatic victories in decades, looking the Chinese in the eye and standing up to their expansionist designs.

In 2020, the Indian troops in eastern Ladakh were engaged in what turned out to be a months-long face-off with the Chinese army along the friction points in Eastern Ladakh. The face-off was a result of Chinese aggression in the region and a unilateral attempt to alter the status quo at the border while India was busy tackling the coronavirus outbreak that had its roots in the Chinese city of Wuhan.

Believing India would have no appetite for a border confrontation amidst the pandemic, the Chinese PLA attempted to clandestinely expand its presence in the border areas and stake a claim on Indian territories. However, the Indian armed forces resisted China's salami-slicing tactics, touching off a stand-off between the armies of the two countries.

On June 15, 2020, a clash between Indian and Chinese troops at <u>Galwan Valley</u> in Ladakh erupted against freezing sub-zero temperatures in the night which escalated border tensions between the two nuclear-armed neighbouring nations. While the Indian government acknowledged the casualties suffered and honoured its soldiers, China has been hiding its casualties in the clash since the very beginning. Even though China has been vague on the number of soldiers it lost in the Galwan clashes, western media outlets assert that 35-40 Chinese soldiers had died in the clashes with their Indian counterparts.

Since then, the tense stand-off between the armies of the two countries along the border in eastern Ladakh has defined India's foreign policy toward China. It has conveyed to Beijing, in no uncertain terms, that India values its territorial integrity and it will not shy away from using militaristic means to counter Chinese aggression along the border regions.

India's strategic ambiguity in Russia's invasion of Ukraine

More recently, India has maintained a measured silence on Russia's war in Ukraine, placing self-interest above the desire to seek validation from the West. While it has attracted the wrath of virtue-signalling leftists and hypocritical western commentariats, who feel outraged that India's foreign policy has not aligned with the West in confronting Russia, India's strategic ambiguity over the issue has ensured that it has not antagonised Russia, one of its oldest and most-reliable defence partners.

Until recently, India bought almost all its frontline arms from Moscow. India's major weapons are overwhelmingly

— about 85% — of Russian origin. In addition to this, the Stockholm International Peace Research Institute says that "new orders [from India] for a variety of Russian arms in 2019–20 ... will probably lead to an increase in Russian arms exports in the coming five years."

Despite the west's sanctions against Russia, India bought more than twice as much crude oil from Russia since it invaded Ukraine as it did in 2021 as New Delhi snapped up discounted Russian oil to fulfil its energy requirements. With inflationary pressures looming and the fuel prices hitting record-high, it was an astute move on the Modi government's part to disregard the western diktats and buy Russian oil available at discounted rates.

With its refusal to toe the western line in the Russia-Ukraine crisis and embrace neutrality, India demonstrated that its foreign policy is rooted in the country's self-interest and not in abiding by the hypocritical standards of morality preached by the West.

Prime Minister Modi has been a powerful figure since he stormed into power in 2014 by winning Lok Sabha election with a massive mandate. In all these years he has clearly delivered a strong message: "We are not here for any positions but for a responsibility". From bureaucrats to MPs, everyone started falling in line. Be it strengthening foreign policy or launching welfare schemes for low-income groups, team Modi has been working day and night to fulfil people's expectations.

The Modi-led government has completed its one tenure and is now serving its second tenure. Let us look at 10 major things that the Modi government has achieved in these 8 years:

1. *Make in India*

To facilitate investment, boost research & development (R&D), ensure product originality and create skill-based jobs by establishing industrial sector; a major national programme was started by Narendra Modi. Modi has reached out to the world with his idea of 'Make in India' and it has generated a positive response from foreign companies. Key Labour Law reform in the pipeline will boost the manufacturing industry and foreign investment in India.

2. *Swachh Bharat Abhiyan (Clean India Campaign)*

Swachh Bharat Abhiyan was launched on October 2, 2014, by Modi. Filth is considered one of the major problems in India and Modi gave the issue its due importance by launching a nationwide campaign. Many called it a masterstroke from Modi as it put him at par with Mahatma Gandhi in public perception and also gave people the message to act on hygiene and civic sense. Modi nominated notable personalities from film industry, sports, media, business, and other celebrities to promote the initiative.

3. *Jan Dhan Yojana*

On 15 August 2014, Modi announced Jan Dhan Yojana. Its main focus has been on reaching every household to provide credit facility, pension, and insurance to account holders. As per the data of the Finance Ministry, a total of 44.23 Jan Dhan accounts have been opened till December 2021.

4. Economic Reforms and Policy Implementation

Modi-led NDA government's primary focus is on reviving the Indian economy through major reforms in the manufacturing and export sector. The government has not only increased the limits of FDI in Railways, Insurance, and Defence but also encouraged privatisation of loss-making public sector companies.

Without being bogged down by coalition partners, Modi persisted with his focus on transformation. On the infrastructure front, government has already begun work on connecting major metros under the Diamond Quadrilateral rail corridor project. Major reforms and developments are under process for Modi's dream projects: 100 Smart Cities and Clean Ganga Mission.

5. Foreign Policy Put on Fast-track Mode

Modi's foreign policy is currently focused on improving relations with neighbouring countries and getting the world to invest in India. In the US, he met several American business leaders and invited them to be a part of Make in India programme. During his visit to France, he urged Airbus, the aerospace giant, to explore manufacturing opportunities in India. While in Germany, he made a strong pitch for the Make in India initiative. He has been trying to send across the message of a more "competitive, confident, and secure" India.

6. Confidence-building Measures in Kashmir

Kashmir is an integral part of India but has a long list of complaints against previous governments – both Centre and state. When the flood created devastations in the valley, the response from the Modi government was immediate and genuine. Modi dedicated constant monitoring system for flood-affected areas and the people of Kashmir. He also decided to spend Deepawali with Kashmir flood survivors. Even his critics praised his move. After a long time, an Indian politician managed to establish a connect with the Kashmiri people.

Even after the abrogation of Article 370 and the conversion of Jammu and Kashmir into two union territories, constant efforts have been made to build confidence among the residents.

7. Mann ki Baat

Mann ki Baat is another big initiative by PM Modi to interact with the general public. It is a radio talk show where the PM talks about a current issue and shares his idea on the same. It is aired officially on All India Radio. From there it is aired and telecasted on various radio and TV channels. Its first episode was aired on October 8, 2014. Till today, a total of 88 episodes have been broadcasted.

8. Ayushman Bharat

Ayushman Bharat is a health insurance scheme launched by PM Modi on September 23, 2018. Under this scheme, every year health coverage of a sum of 5 lakh rupees each will be given to all the beneficiary families. This scheme will cover over 10 crore families who are poor. Till April 2021, 75,532 Ayushman Bharat Health and Wellness Centres were made operational, and 44.24 crore people got treated there. By December 2022, the government is aiming to set up 1.5 lakh Ayushman Bharat Health and Wellness Centres in India.

9. *Digital India*

Digital India was another big initiative by PM Modi that helped in the development of India. With an increase in internet users every day due to the availability of more data at low prices led to the launch of the Digital India Programme. Through this programme many websites were launched for the ease of the citizens. United Payment Interface (UPI) was also a part of this initiative.

10. *Atmanirbhar Bharat- Vocal for Local*

PM Modi looked at COVID-19 as a way to create an opportunity for the local products. That's when he emphasized the importance of being 'Atmanirbhar' and urged people to be Vocal for Local. It was done with the aim to promote the local vendors so that they can survive during the economic crisis created due to the pandemic

Prime Minister Narendra Modi's NDA government has completed eight years of 'Seva, Sushasan and Garib Kalyan'. These eight years have been dedicated to working for the welfare of the poor, facilitating the middle class, empowering women, implementing pro-farmer policies, creating educational and job opportunities for our youth, ensuring social justice and developing every region of India. PM Modi has brought the politics of development - Vikasvaad - into the mainstream, making it the focal point around which political discourse and policy action revolves.

Since assuming office in 2014, PM Modi has remained firm in his resolve of keeping 'India first' in every policy formulation and action. The government has guarded India's borders, ensured internal security, and consistently promoted our interests abroad. From the digital revolution to the elimination of open defecation, from vaccinating the entire eligible population through indigenous vaccines to increasing defence exports, government has guarded India's borders, ensured internal security, and consistently promoted our interests abroad. From the digital revolution to the elimination of open defecation, from vaccinating the entire eligible population through indigenous vaccines to increasing defence exports, significantly, over the last eight years India has successfully achieved what was essentially considered unimaginable in the past. These last eight years have witnessed a paradigm shift in public service delivery and the implementation of government schemes and infrastructure projects. From the completion of infrastructure projects delayed by decades to the provision of basic facilities that earlier governments failed to provide, there has been a turnaround in governance in India. The government has ensured irreversible empowerment for various marginalised groups, helping them become self-reliant by providing a social safety net. In stark contrast to piece-meal delivery of the past, the Prime Minister has always focused on ensuring that no one is left behind and unable to access basic facilities. The massive expansion of welfare coverage over the last eight years has allowed India to finally aspire to achieve 100% saturation. Saturation coverage of the benefits of good governance ends politics of discrimination and corruption that used to be played by providing benefits to some while denying the same to others. Adopting stiff targets considered almost impossible to achieve earlier, and fulfilling them on time, has become the new normal under PM Modi's leadership. India has transformed from being a mere onlooker to a global leader in various spheres. In New India, development does not involve trade-offs related to the environment – both go hand in hand. Over the last eight years, the government has given due recognition to Indian culture and values and promoted India's rich civilisational heritage across the globe. After first assuming an elected office in 2001 as Chief Minister of Gujarat and then going on to become the Prime Minister, in the past twenty years, Narendra Modi has set a new benchmark in reforms and governance which has become a model not just in India but in many parts of the world. He has not only encouraged people to aspire but also provided adequate government support for fulfilling their rising aspirations. He has also inspired the nation by encouraging everyone to think of the next twenty-five years as the 'Amrit Kaal' for building a strong, prosperous and inclusive India.

I t was extremely distressing that even after several decades since independence even basic facilities such as banking, toilets, LPG cylinders, tap water connections, electricity connections, healthcare, etc. have not been provided to the citizens. These facilities that should have been provided to all citizens in the previous century itself are finally reaching all Indians in the 21st century due to Prime Minister Narendra Modi's tireless efforts. The umbrella of welfare schemes started by the Modi government in 2014 has successfully ensured widespread access to basic facilities for most Indians. The Modi government has ensured that citizens, irrespective of their caste, religion, gender, region, economic class, or political preferences, received their entitled benefits. As the government has shifted focus to saturation, soon, all Indians will have access to these basic facilities. Saturation coverage of basic facilities has been the hallmark of the endeavour of the Modi government. The Modi government has successfully managed to plug leakages in public service delivery. The government's efforts to extend welfare provisioning and poverty alleviation have received recognition from global institutions. A recent IMF paper has credited the Modi government for ending extreme poverty in the country. Various programmes of the Modi government have empowered marginalised groups such as Scheduled Castes, Scheduled Tribes, and Other Backward Classes. PM Modi's approach towards social justice has centred around irreversible empowerment. This ensures individuals from marginalised groups become self-reliant and selfsufficient rather than remaining dependent on the political establishment for their needs. Programmes such as MUDRA Yojana and Stand Up India are creating a large pool of young entrepreneurs from marginalised groups. These individuals not only achieve better lives for their respective families but also become an inspiration for others within their respective communities. The Modi government's historic decision to provide reservations for economically weaker sections provided much-needed support to poor households. Creating a new category meant that this extension of benefits did not reduce benefits already extended to other marginalised groups. The government has corrected past wrongs and ensured the long-pending rights of marginalised groups. For instance, the government's decision to implement OBC and EWS reservations in all India quota seats in medical education. This will ensure that students from these groups can also aspire to become doctors in affordable government colleges. The work done on empowering Divyangjan, transgenders, Denotified and Nomadic tribes, and other such hitherto unserved or underserved groups is also noteworthy. An integral element of PM Modi's policy has been the effort to recognize icons of social empowerment. This builds self-pride among communities by highlighting their contribution to nationbuilding. For instance, the government has declared November 15 of every year as Janjatiya Gaurav Divas to commemorate the sacrifices of brave tribal fighters for the country. Such recognition increases the self-confidence of various communities and strengthens their resolve to work for the country's progress.

Irreversible empowerment for marginalised groups · Earlier, the attitude of certain governments was to patronise the marginalised groups by ensuring some piecemeal benefits. · They wanted to keep the people dependent on them, and hence, irreversible empowerment was denied. · But now, PM Modi has ensured a shift from patronage-based support to irreversible empowerment. · Schemes like Stand Up India and MUDRA Yojana are empowering individuals from marginalised groups by providing entrepreneurship opportunities. · These entrepreneurs will shape aspirations and become role models for the entire community. Ending the politics of low expectations and low delivery · Once a gas connection is given, an electricity connection is given or a tap water connection is given, none can take it away. · Further, the poor become aspirational and have higher expectations since their basic needs are met. · This creates greater expectations from governments and pushes them to deliver more. · For a long time, India was harmed by politics of low delivery and low expectations. But now, that is being changed by PM Modi.

For Farmers

Over the last eight years, Indian agriculture has touched new heights due to Prime Minister Narendra Modi's Beej Se Bazar Tak approach. The government has focused on protecting farmers from various risks, extending income support, improving access to information, and building forward linkages. This has led to the modernization of Indian agriculture and a substantial increase in farmer incomes. Since 2014, the Modi government has taken multiple measures to make farming in India less risky by building a safety net for farmers and reducing their dependence on rainfall for irrigation. Earlier, an extended dry spell or crop damage after just a few days of untimely rains would drive lakhs of farmers into heavy indebtedness. The Pradhan Mantri Fasal Bima Yojana changed this status quo. Launched in 2016, the scheme overhauled the agriculture insurance system and has provided a much-needed safety net for farmers. The PM Krishi Sinchayee Yojana has expanded irrigation coverage and reduced farmers' dependence on rainfall for irrigation. Record production and consequent increase in procurement by the government have led to an unprecedented rise in farm incomes. Moreover, the gradual transition towards payment to farmers through DBT has protected farmers from unfair charges and commissions charged by intermediaries. In 2019, the government launched the PM Kisan Samman Nidhi to provide an assured cash transfer of Rs. 6,000 per year to farmers. This supplemental income received through regular instalments has enabled even small farmers to purchase better quality inputs, improve their land productivity, and increase their income. Indian farmers are steadily transitioning towards 'smart' farming as useful scientific information and the latest innovations in agriculture are being made available to them. Rich insights from soil health cards issued by the government have helped farmers make efficient use of various inputs and maximize their yield. Through multiple programmes, small farmers are being encouraged to adopt natural and organic farming. This has led to lower investments on inputs, higher farm incomes and protection from the perils of climate change and various uncertainties. Strengthening forward linkages of agriculture is necessary for improving the condition of farmers. Linking agriculture markets throughout the country through the e-NAM initiative has brought transparency and increased competition in agriculture markets. This has not only enabled farmers to get better prices for their yield but also reduced price distortions that hampered consumer interests. The Production Linked Incentive (PLI) scheme for food processing industries is a turning point for Indian agriculture as there will be a massive increase in domestic demand for farm produce. The steady increase in farm yields and stability of Indian farmers over the last eight years has brought a paradigm shift in Indian agriculture. Today, Indian farmers aren't producing for just self-consumption or sale in the domestic market. Instead, they seek to export their products and feed the world.

Nari shakti

Prime Minister Narendra Modi considers womenled development a central dimension of India's progress and necessary for strengthening India. In the last eight years, the Modi government has launched numerous welfare schemes that have aimed to empower women and make them lead India's development journey. These programmes have provided much-desired assistance to women at various stages in their lives. They have also unshackled

Indian women and freed them from the drudgery they experienced in daily life. However, rather than merely limiting his role to the distribution of state-led welfare benefits, PM Modi is using the power of mass movements to bring about social transformation. His efforts are enabling women to overcome social barriers and fulfil their aspirations. The Modi government has taken a remarkable lifecyclebased approach towards women empowerment. A wide range of government programmes assist women at various stages - from childhood to adulthood and even during old-age - to ensure their safety and empowerment. At every step, opportunities are opened up to help increase women's choices as well as empower them to take those decisions to their logical conclusion. Mission Poshan fulfils the nutritional requirements of children, adolescent girls, pregnant women, and lactating mothers. One Stop Centres (OSCs) assist women in distress. The Pradhan Mantri Matru Vandana Yojana (PMMVY) and Pradhan Mantri Surakshit Matritva Abhiyan (PMSMA) incentivize institutional deliveries and regular health check-ups for pregnant women and lactating mothers. The impact of this approach has been evident in many outcomes, such as an improved sex ratio at birth, a rise in institutional deliveries, declining infant mortality, and a lower maternal mortality rate. Programmes such as MUDRA Yojana have allowed crores of women across the country to pursue micro-level entrepreneurship and become financially independent. PM Modi has made unshackling women and freeing them from the drudgery of everyday life a key objective of policymaking. Every flagship welfare scheme launched by the Modi government has improved the lives of women across the country. LPG cylinders under the Ujjwala Yojana have saved crores of women from chronic respiratory disorders through smoke-free kitchens and ended the daily ordeal of collecting firewood for cooking. Due to the Swachh Bharat Abhiyan, crores of women can access toilets at their convenience without any fear over safety or violation of dignity. Walking long distances to collect water for daily consumption is becoming history as households across the county are getting private tap water connections under the Jal Jeevan Mission. As owners of the family home received under PM Awas Yojana, women are becoming active participants in household decision-making. Since 2014, PM Modi has been a pillar of support and encouragement for Indian women in their quest to break innumerable barriers, open new doors for themselves, and fulfil their aspirations. In the last 8 years, there has been a massive increase in women police personnel. In 2018, PM Modi announced a landmark decision to allow permanent commission for women in the armed forces. Across diverse fields, women are taking the lead in India's rise, from sports to academics to performing arts.

For youth

Prime Minister Narendra Modi's unmatched connect with the country's youth has ensured that the government has been able to not only fulfil their aspirations but also harness immense talent for national progress. Today's youth see nothing as unattainable and aspire to make India a global leader in unchartered territories that earlier generations usually avoided. Rather than dismissing their 'can do spirit,' the Prime Minister has consistently created a conducive environment through an enabling policy framework. Unlike earlier generations that used to aspire for salaried jobs, a large segment of today's youth seeks to explore selfemployment opportunities. In multiple addresses since 2014, the Prime Minister has encouraged the Indian youth to pursue their desire to start entrepreneurial ventures and become job creators rather than just job seekers. His encouragement has played an instrumental role in creating a critical attitudinal shift in society, the cornerstone of the success of India's startup ecosystem. Today, youngsters are willing to take risks to fulfil their dreams. They know that PM Modi will provide constant support in their endeavour. Through the Startup India programme launched in 2016, the Modi government has taken numerous measures to promote startups and entrepreneurship. This includes tax exemptions, easing regulations, and reducing the compliance burden. Like entrepreneurship, sports was considered a forbidden field for most youngsters. It used to be viewed merely as a leisure activity, and parents usually discouraged children from professionally pursuing sports. PM Modi brought a crucial mindset change and introduced various policies that have allowed innumerable youngsters to fulfil their dream of pursuing sports as a career. India saw its best performance ever in the Tokyo Olympics and Paralympics recently. This has been an outcome of long-term planning and support through the flagship TOPS programme. World class education and skill development opportunities being created by the Modi government are empowering our youth and contributing to the collective dream of building a strong labour force. In the last eight years, record numbers of new IITs, IIMs, medical colleges, and universities have been opened across the country Since its launch, more than 1.34 crore youngsters have received skill training under the PM Kaushal Vikas Yojana and improved their employability. The National Education Policy (NEP) approved in 2020 is bringing a paradigm shift in the Indian education system through much needed and longpending reforms in school and higher education. The Modi government has focused on providing meaningful employment to the Indian youth that enables them to achieve a better life for their family. India has become a preferred destination for investment, and employment opportunities are being created for crores of young Indians. The massive rise in new EPFO accounts confirms the Modi government's success in creating new formal jobs. Consistent efforts to assist MSMEs and programmes such as Production Linked Incentive Scheme for domestic production have contributed towards job creation. The record exports achieved in 2021-22 have taken job creation and hiring to a positivity level that is better than even the pre-pandemic years! Moreover, the current unemployment level is lower than the prepandemic levels indicating new employment opportunities for crores of youngsters.

For middle class

Since 2014, ease of living in everyday life is becoming a reality for households across the country, be it in urban areas or rural, be it poor or the middle class. From welfare programmes to infrastructure investment, from modifying government processes to introducing protective regulation, ease of living for citizens has been the central objective of policymaking under the Modi government. Prime Minister Narendra Modi has ensured that ease of living has ceased to remain a privilege of a few. The Modi government has assured that citizens across all segments of the society have access to basic facilities such as banking, LPG connections, sanitation, electricity, tap water, and affordable healthcare. Government programmes for providing these facilities are ensuring that India's aspirational class experiences a significant improvement in the quality of daily life over the last eight years. Today, a smokefree kitchen or uninterrupted power supply is a reality rather than just a dream for most households in the country. Lower taxation and affordable borrowing rates have led to massive savings for middle-class households and expanded their disposable income. Positive changes in income tax exemptions and direct tax reforms have reduced their tax burden and made tax filing simpler for the middle class. The Goods and Services Tax has led to a decline in a wide range of everyday expenses for consumers. From items of daily household consumption to leisure activities such as eating out in restaurants, affordability has increased after the introduction of the GST. Crores of urban middleclass households are fulfilling their lifelong dream of owning a house. A sharp reduction in interest rates and the Modi government's Credit Linked Subsidy Scheme under PM Awas Yojana have enabled people to buy their first home. Alongside this, strengthening the regulatory framework through steps such as the formation of the Real Estate Regulatory Authority (RERA) has ensured that the lifetime earnings of citizens are protected by a legal framework that upholds the rights of homebuyers. Prime Minister Narendra Modi's big push on infrastructure since 2014 has also helped middle-class households reduce expenditure. The UDAN programme has provided air connectivity to numerous tier 2 and tier 3 cities and ensured that air travel isn't limited to the affluent. Travelling by train isn't the default option for middle-class households anymore as the UDAN scheme has made air travel more affordable. In the last eight years, a record number of metro rail projects have been approved and commissioned in numerous cities. As a result, citizens are now shifting from private vehicles to public transportation and making considerable savings without compromising on comfort. The Digital India initiative has made the government more accessible and transparent to citizens. Now, citizens can access hundreds of services provided by central and state governments at the click of a button through the UMANG app. Apps like Digilocker have removed the need to carry physical copies of documents. Through various steps for ease of living, the Modi government is transforming the daily life of Indian citizens, removing routine worries and raising their quality of life.

Infrastructure

Over the last eight years, India has taken a crucial step towards becoming a global economic powerhouse by building worldclass infrastructure. The Modi government has completed numerous infrastructure projects that were hitherto considered unachievable due to inordinate delays and other constraints. A trade-off between speed and scale is history as timely completion of public works projects has become a norm rather than an exception under Prime Minister Narendra Modi's leadership. Thinking big and delivering without delay have been hallmarks of infrastructure development under the Modi government. PM Modi's active role has made the infrastructure turnaround possible. Rather than merely announcing new projects, the Prime Minister has regularly monitored the progress of projects through the PRAGATI platform. This led to the successful completion of various long-delayed projects. The last eight years have witnessed a remarkable improvement in connectivity in the country. The daily average highway construction reached an all-time high and has consistently remained far higher than pre-2014 levels. Similarly, a rapid increase in the construction of rural roads has made access to roads nearly universal in the hinterland. Indian railways has also witnessed a massive capacity expansion in the last eight years through line doubling and electrification of railway tracks. In just eight years, the Modi government has built and operationalised 66 airports and ensured air connectivity to innumerable tier 2 and tier 3 cities. Metro rail is not limited to metropolitan cities anymore. In the last eight years, metro rail projects have reached 18 cities. Improved connectivity has proven to be a game-changer for the Indian economy. It has facilitated commerce and unlocked the economic potential of numerous towns and cities. Also, connectivity has reduced costs and logistical hurdles for Indian enterprises. Prime Minister Narendra Modi has often suggested that connectivity in the digital age isn't limited to physical connectivity. Digital connectivity and IT infrastructure have become critical determinants of economic growth. To unleash the power of high-speed internet, the government has now resolved to connect all six lakh plus villages. The Pradhan Mantri Gati Shakti Masterplan announced by Prime Minister Narendra Modi demonstrates a new vision for a new India. This is the most extensive plan for infrastructure development in the history of independent India, as the government plans to invest nearly Rs. 100 lakh crore in the coming years. Integrated long-term planning under Gati Shakti will improve last-mile connectivity and multi-modal connectivity across the country and bolster India's economic progress for many decades. Rather than taking a myopic project-based approach, the master plan provides a comprehensive strategy for infrastructure development in the country. The lack of coordinated planning has led to massive wastage of public resources in the past. The new infrastructure will make India one of the leaders in the global supply chain and ensure that it remains the world's most preferred destination for investment. Gati Shakti will also lead to the creation of a large number of direct and indirect jobs since infrastructure is known to be a job-intensive sector.

Health care

The Covid pandemic has been the most significant public health challenge for any government since independence. Despite the stiff challenge, India not only remained resilient and managed an effective response but also emerged as a global role model. Prime Minister Narendra Modi's remarkable leadership and consistent efforts by the government since 2014 to augment India's healthcare capacity helped the country successfully fight the pandemic. The Modi government undertook a science-based approach for managing the pandemic. In early 2020, when many global leaders refused to even consider Covid to be a serious threat, India had already initiated its Covid management policy. For instance, even before a single Covid case was reported in the country, India had started screening travellers arriving from abroad. Moreover, realising that essential supplies for pandemic management required coordination across various sectors, Prime Minister Narendra Modi adopted a 'whole of government' approach. This ensured that various government departments worked simultaneously and coordinated their actions. The paradigm shift in India's healthcare system since 2014 was visible during the pandemic. Accessible and affordable quality healthcare has become a reality for citizens. Earlier, medical expenditure used to be a severe economic burden for low-income households and often led them into debt traps. In 2018, the Modi government gave a permanent relief from this burden to around 18 crore households by launching the Ayushman Bharat - Pradhan Mantri Jan Arogya Yojana, the world's largest health insurance programme. The government's telemedicine programme - eSanjeevani, bridges the urban-rural divide in access to specialist doctors. The Jan Aushadhi Kendras, located in more than 700 districts, provide quality generic medicines to citizens at affordable rates. The government has overhauled the country's immunisation programme by launching Mission Indradhanush, which has protected an entire generation from diseases that could have led to massive expenditure on medical treatment. The Modi government has brought a crucial turnaround in medical education. Few government colleges, high fees in private medical colleges, and massive corruption in seat allocation had severely limited opportunities for medical education earlier. In the last eight years, the Modi government has approved/ established 15 AIIMS and innumerable new medical colleges. Further, the government's bold decision to replace the Medical Council of India with the National Medical Commission has ended corruption in medical education. In 'New India,' a talented student from a humble background in the hinterland can fulfil her dream of becoming a doctor. In the past year, India has successfully rolled out the world's largest vaccination drive ever. This marks a landmark change for India. In the past, the country has had to wait for decades and lose innumerable lives before starting vaccination. Until now, more than 1.9 billion doses of Covid vaccine have been administered across the country. It is a historic achievement that India has been able to conduct this massive exercise entirely through indigenous vaccines. The Modi government's multi-dimensional outlook covering preventive and curative healthcare has led to an improvement in individual wellness rather than merely improving health outcomes.

National security

The Modi government won the people's hearts in 2014 with a simple yet powerful mantra of putting 'India first.' From protecting our nation's borders to giving a befitting response to our adversaries, from promoting India's interests abroad to safeguarding Indians settled abroad, Prime Minister Narendra Modi's decisions have consistently reflected his promise of 'India First'. The Prime Minister's zero tolerance for terrorism has ensured that the country is much safer today. In stark contrast to the earlier era, when our citizens used to be under attack at will, our citizens feel much more secure. Over the last eight years, India has made terrorism a significant issue on global platforms and taken the lead in the world's battle against terrorism. Under PM Modi's leadership, India is getting accustomed to taking giant strides rather than small steps. This spirit of 'New India' is reflected in our rapidly rising defence production and exports. From being a country that was heavily dependent on imports for even basic weapons and defence equipment, India is moving towards becoming selfreliant in defence production. Defence exports have increased over 6-fold in the last eight years, and India is exporting defence equipment and weapons to many countries. This success has been possible due to government efforts such as providing appropriate incentives for defence production, enabling foreign investment, and building defence industrial corridors. The defence industry is emerging as one of the most vibrant sectors of the Indian economy. In the last eight years, innumerable new jobs have been created in the industry, and the surge in exports has helped in improving India's trade deficit. Moreover, selfreliance in defence production also strengthens our diplomatic interests across the globe. There has been an unprecedented strengthening of India's position abroad in the last eight years. India's voice is now being heard and respected by countries across the globe. From climate change to international conflicts, from terrorism to global trade, the world is eagerly looking towards India for its views and solutions. Since 2014, Indian diaspora located across the globe has felt assured that PM Modi is always looking out for their safety and wellbeing. They know that if an adverse situation arises, the Indian government will leave no stone unturned to protect them. In the past year, the government ensured the safe evacuation of hundreds of stranded Indians in Afghanistan under Operation Devi Shakti. As a guardian of Indic culture and traditions, the government ensured that swaroops of the Guru Granth Sahib were safely brought to India. Earlier this year, when hundreds of Indian students were stranded in Ukraine after the Russian attack, India launched Operation Ganga to rescue them safely. From overcoming logistical hurdles to using diplomatic channels, the Modi government has consistently gone to great lengths to ensure its citizens' safety.

Economy

The global Covid-19 pandemic since 2020 had a severe economic fallout and affected all countries across the globe. While many economies continue to struggle with sluggish economic growth and record-breaking inflation, India remains the sole bright spot. This has been recognized by global institutions such as the IMF and World Bank which have forecasted India to be the fastest-growing country among major economies in the world. Various indicators of economic performance, from GST revenues to manufacturing activity, indicate that the Indian economy has not only bounced back but even breached prepandemic levels. The Modi government's comprehensive approach for managing the economic fallout of the pandemic ensured minimal effects and swift recovery. The government's Aatmanirbhar Bharat plan turned the crisis into an opportunity and gave muchneeded impetus to economic growth. The swift recovery can be attributed to extending adequate support to various sectors of the economy and a string of structural reforms since 2014. These reforms strengthened the Indian economy and enabled it to withstand the drastic effects of the pandemic. The Modi government's dynamic FDI policy has made India the preferred global destination for investment. Moreover, numerous decisions for improving the ease of doing business have promoted both domestic and foreign investment. Unlike earlier governments, the Modi government has made MSMEs, a central focus of its economic policy. The government's Emergency Credit Line Guarantee Scheme during the Covid pandemic protected more than one crore MSMEs and saved them from possible permanent closure. Moreover, reforms such as revision of MSME definition and changes in labour and environment laws have allowed MSMEs to expand their operations and grow. PM Modi's clarion calls for 'Make in India' and building an Aatmanirbhar Bharat have led to a transformation of India's manufacturing sector. This has also given a huge boost to our exports which have crossed more than $400 billion for the first time in the country's history. The Production Linked Incentives (PLI) schemes have led to a turnaround in numerous sectors of the economy. From a net importer earlier, India has become a manufacturing hub for mobile phones and is annually exporting mobile phones worth more than $5.5 billion. PLI Schemes across 14 sectors have created lakhs of jobs and placed the Indian economy on a rapid growth trajectory.

PM Modi has consistently assured the country's wealth creators adequate support in their efforts towards innovation and making India self-reliant. This is reflected in his personal focus and support for the Indian Semiconductor Mission (ISM) and its vision of building a semiconductor and display manufacturing ecosystem in India. This will make India one of the few countries with such manufacturing capabilities and further boost economic wellbeing and job creation. Global acknowledgement of India's economic progress is visible in numerous countries' desire to quickly finalize trade deals with India. The dream of a digital economy is becoming a reality. Over the last few years, UPI has already become the preferred mode of payment. From street vendors to luxury stores, from Dhabas to fivestar hotels, everyone is using UPI for making and accepting payments. Cashless transactions not only improve ease of living but also expand formalisation of the economy.

Ease of doing business

Prime Minister Narendra Modi's vision of making India an attractive investment destination and the transformative reforms over the last eight years led to a historic improvement in ease of doing business and an unprecedented rise in foreign direct investment. This is not only supporting existing enterprises but also encouraging a new wave of risk-taking, be it among small entrepreneurs or new start-ups. Rather than being merely an urban phenomenon, start-up culture has now spread to all parts of the country. Since 2014, rent-seeking and red-tapism have been replaced by a red carpet. The government is not an obstacle in the path of risktakers but is an active enabler. Entrepreneurs and investors in India are now delighted by a business-friendly environment and a government that actively addresses their concerns and redresses grievances. This paradigm shift has been made possible through landmark decisions such as removing retrospective taxation and Angel Tax. The Prime Minister's mantra of transparency and reducing compliance requirements demonstrates a government that trusts its citizens. This trust is being reciprocated in the rising number of taxpayers and record tax collections. Meanwhile, the tax cuts have increased the investible surplus available to companies. Similarly, promoting self-regulation, self-certification, computerised random labour inspections and faceless assessment/appeal in taxes has not only dealt a blow to 'Inspector Raj' but also improved compliance. The National Single Window System allows obtaining all approvals through a single platform. Moreover, the Modi government has reduced unnecessary compliance burden by repealing more than 1,400 archaic laws and nearly 25,000 compliances. These used to create unnecessary costs and hurdles for Indian enterprises. From the ease of starting a business to ease of getting electricity, from labour reforms such as the new labour codes to the decriminalisation of many sections of the Companies Act, the gamut of different steps taken firmly establish that the environment for wealth creators is the best that it has ever been. Never before has India witnessed such enthusiasm for entrepreneurship and start-ups. The number of new government-recognized startups annually has increased by almost 19 times between 2016- 17 and 2021-22. India's efforts to improve the ease of doing business are being acknowledged on the global stage. This is evident in consistent improvement in various international rankings. For instance, the country's ranking in the World Bank's Ease of Doing Business Index surged from 142 in 2014 to

63 in 2019. Apart from numerous reforms and landmark decisions, Prime Minister Narendra Modi has successfully led a mindset transformation. Unlike previous governments, the Modi government not only considers entrepreneurs as wealth creators but also as partners in national development. Concerted efforts to improve the Ease of Doing Business have led to a historic expansion in the pool of wealth creators. This has increased resources available to the government for poverty alleviation and infrastructure creation. Further, lower compliance costs not only lead to greater earnings for firms but also higher incomes for employees and more hiring.

Changes of policy

The government's Northeast policy has successfully changed the region's economic landscape and has also brought hearts closer. Apart from responsiveness to the needs of the people, this has been made possible by improving physical connectivity and making the region's interests and policy priorities salient to the central government. Earlier, the Northeast was never considered mainstream and repeatedly side-lined in policymaking. This was evident in the number of visits by earlier Prime Ministers and members of their Cabinet to the region. Over the last eight years, Delhi itself has reached the doorstep of the Northeast through regular visits by the Prime Minister, his ministerial colleagues, and senior bureaucrats. The Prime Minister has himself become an ambassador of Northeast culture as he proudly wears traditional attire from the region in public meetings. Through him, the Northeastern culture has reached the entire country and beyond. Various states in the Northeast have faced severe internal security challenges for decades. Under the Modi government, the centre has seriously tackled these challenges and saved innumerable lives through proactive response. The signing of peace accords has led to peace and a decline in violence in the region. These efforts have paved the way for reducing AFSPA coverage in the region. Long pending disputes between various states in the Northeast had been a major concern in the region. Many decades-long disputes are finally getting permanently resolved through the active efforts of the Modi government. This will give a further boost to integration and trust and pave the way forward for long-term peace and progress. Lack of physical connectivity and poor infrastructure had contributed to the Northeast's isolation for many decades. Innumerable long-pending infrastructure projects were completed and delivered to the public in the last eight years. The long list of projects includes iconic projects such as Bogibeel Bridge, inaugurated by PM Modi in 2018, sixteen years after its announcement by PM Atal Bihari Vajpayee. Even basic railway connectivity was lacking in the region until the Modi government took it up on a mission mode. Over the last eight years, the Modi government has focused on expanding the railway network in the region. The Modi government has extended unprecedented support for reviving traditional sectors of the economy in the region. The landmark decision to declare Bamboo as grass and the launch of the National Bamboo Mission gave a fresh impetus to the production of Bamboo based products in the region. On numerous occasions, Prime Minister Narendra Modi has highlighted the success of Sikkim in promoting organic farming and becoming the world's first 100% organic state. From being on the margins of the India story, the Northeast is quickly becoming one of the country's growth engines.

CONSERVING CULTURAL HERITAGE

India's cultural traditions and rich heritage have never got the prominence they got in the last 8 years. Prime Minister Narendra Modi takes pride in the country's rich civilizational history and gives due recognition to the cultural heritage. The Modi government is deeply aware of the nation's rich culture and has taken much-needed steps for preserving our heritage. After decades of neglect, various sites of civilizational significance have been redeveloped and revived through the efforts of the Modi government. The Kashi Vishwanath Corridor and various other projects in Varanasi have transformed the by lanes, ghats, and temple complexes in the city. The 900 km Chardham road project will provide seamless allweather road connectivity to the four holy Dhams. PM Modi personally monitored the progress of redevelopment projects in Kedarnath, a temple extremely close to his heart. The newly unveiled statue of Adi Shankaracharya in the Kedarnath complex will be an eternal symbol of civilizational and cultural unity across regions. In August 2020, PM Modi participated in the Bhoomipujan for the Ram Mandir in Ayodhya, a memorable moment in the history of modern India. Bringing back the nation's lost heritage has been a priority for the Modi government. Over centuries, innumerable priceless artefacts, some with deep cultural and religious significance, had been stolen and smuggled abroad. The Modi government adopted a proactive approach for 'bringing back our gods'. On numerous foreign visits, PM Modi discussed this matter with global leaders and multilateral institutions. Today, innumerable countries are themselves reaching out to India to send back stolen artefacts and antiquities. India's efforts have, in fact, inspired similar efforts in Africa and other parts of the globe. PM Modi has successfully initiated a global movement. The Modi government has extended special recognition to a wide range of nation-builders. The Statue of Unity in Gujarat, the world's largest statue, has not only put Kevadia on the global tourism map but also become a spot for remembering the man who delivered national unity. Projects such as revamp of the Jallianwala Bagh complex and the development of sites related to Dr. B.R. Ambedkar as 'Paanchteerth' will etch the sacrifices and achievements of our nationbuilders and freedom fighters in public memory. The Modi government has given recognition to all national heroes irrespective of their politics or ideology. This is best showcased in the newly inaugurated Pradhan Mantri Sangrahalaya, a museum in Delhi celebrating the lives and contributions of all Prime Ministers of India. Innumerable bravehearts have lost their lives while protecting Bharat Mata. In 2019, Prime Minister Narendra Modi inaugurated the National War Memorial in New Delhi which remembers those who made the supreme sacrifice for the country. Though it had been under consideration since 1961, not much progress was made in this crucial project. Prime Minister Narendra Modi gave much-needed momentum to this project and work started after approval in 2015.

POWERED INDIA

Prime Minister Narendra Modi is India's first techsavvy Prime Minister. A tech-enthusiast since his youth, he has made technology and digital solutions central to governance. In Gujarat first, and now in India, he has worked on bridging the digital divide, democratising technology and bringing rapid digitalization of governance. In the last eight years, there has been a meteoric rise in mobile ownership across India. The sharp decline in the cost of data has led to deep penetration of the internet, bridging the urban-rural divide. Technology adoption by the government over the last eight years has ensured a remarkable increase in transparency in governance. Today, all government programmes have a digital dashboard that provides all details of beneficiaries. These dashboards have enabled citizens to hold the government accountable and considerably reduced leakages in public service delivery. Digital delivery of public services is eliminating corruption and promoting ease of living. From Direct Benefits Transfer to faceless tax assessments, reducing discretion is eliminating rent seeking tendencies in the officialdom and empowering citizens. Technology has also made governance in India more efficient and effective. From the adoption of biometric authentication to the creation of digital single-window approval systems, governance is undergoing a paradigm shift in India. The Modi government has effectively deployed technology and digital tools for ensuring transparency and plugging leakages in governance. For example, the introduction of Direct Benefits Transfer and Aadhar authentication in various welfare scams have led to the elimination of lakhs of ghost beneficiaries, enormous savings for the government, and timely delivery of benefits to citizens. In 2021-22, the government saved more than Rs. 2 lakh crore due to the distribution of benefits through DBT. Even public procurement, a common avenue for bureaucratic corruption earlier, has now become digital as the Government e-Marketplace (GeM) portal is being utilized by government departments and PSUs for their procurement. The portal is successfully eliminating corruption and streamlining public procurement in the country. The rapid digitalization has also been an opportunity to unlock India's economic potential and fulfil the aspirations of millions of entrepreneurs. Innumerable tech-based start-ups across the country have been facilitated through various programmes such as Start Up India. Under PM Modi, technology is being democratized. The programme to take optic fibre to every Gram Panchayat in the country is running at full steam. The cost of data is affordable. The digital divide is going to be a thing of the past as all segments of the country are actively using modern technology - from digital payments to communication. India is becoming a digital economy as UPI has become the preferred mode of payment for all merchants - from the local vegetable market to the biggest mall in the city. Digital delivery of vaccines through the CoWIN platform allowed India to ensure equity and accessibility in vaccine distribution. India is leading a global revolution for digitalization. Other countries are looking towards India for providing tech solutions such as the CoWIN platform. As a responsible country, India is ensuring open-source access to these digital tools and supporting developing countries in their transition towards digitalization.

ENVIRONMENT AND SUSTAINABILITY

From the times of Chief Minister Narendra Modi to Prime Minister Narendra Modi, one consistent theme in governance is the illustration that development and environmental conservation can go handin-hand. Under PM Modi's leadership, there has been rapid development without hurting the environment and, in fact, while protecting it. Over the last eight years, India has emerged as a global leader in the fight against climate change. From negotiations over global climate change deals to the adoption of renewable energy, India is leading international efforts for environmental protection and shaping the global agenda When PM Modi took over in

2014, India was globally seen as a roadblock in climate negotiations. However, the Prime Minister has given solutions to forge a path forward. Since COP 21, the Prime Minister's principle of climate justice has ensured that equity concerns aren't ignored in climate change negotiations. India has remained focused on providing a 'fair deal'. It has ensured that advanced economies cannot abdicate their responsibility towards environmental protection. At the same time, India is also meeting ambitious climate goals. At the COP 26 at Glasglow last year, PM Modi shared his five-point agenda - 'Panchamrit,' for countering climate change. This provides a comprehensive approach that most countries can replicate. India's global efforts have been accompanied by consistent steps within the country by the Modi government. The Modi government has brought transparency and objectivity to environmental law compliance. This has not only generated trust in the government but also helped in ensuring that sustainable development becomes possible. The government's remarkable efforts for environmental protection have led to many commendable achievements. There has been a significant increase in forest cover in the country. Over the past decade, the tiger population in India has more than doubled. While many countries fail to fulfil their climate targets, India has hit targets long before deadlines. For example, the target for achieving 40% of installed electricity capacity from nonfossil sources, which was set at COP 21, was fulfilled nine years ahead of schedule. The Namami Gange programme, a flagship initiative of the government, has successfully arrested pollution of the holy river and improved water quality at numerous locations. This cause has been extremely close to PM Modi's heart, as evident in his decision to donate all proceeds from an auction of gifts he received to the Namami Gange programme. The last eight years have witnessed a rapid transition towards renewable sources of energy. India has had the fastest growth rate in renewable energy capacity addition among large economies. Numerous incentives for the renewable energy sector and lower cost of inputs have led to a massive decrease in renewable energy tariffs. Further, the UJALA programme has led to thousands of crores of savings while reducing carbon dioxide emissions. People's participation has been central to the Prime Minister's vision of providing a clean and healthy environment. From cleanliness to avoiding single-use plastic, he has often encouraged citizens to make lifestyle changes to contribute to the environment. By transforming these causes into mass movements, he has ensured impact at scale rather than a temporary shift in public habits.

How bjp reformed after modi

ABSTRACT In the last five years, the Bharatiya Janata Party (BJP) has undergone a massive transformation and is today the country's most formidable political force. The party won the 2014 general election with a convincing majority under the leadership of Prime Minister Narendra Modi who assumed power in May 2014. Today the BJP is in power in 20 states, either on its own or with its allies. This rise can be attributed to various factors, including the party leadership, organisational skills, and effective ground work. This brief analyses the journey of the BJP. In ve years since 2013, when Narendra Modi was declared its prime ministerial candidate, the Bharatiya Janata Party (BJP) has managed to widen its geographical reach and strengthen its electoral and political supremacy across the country. Today, the BJP is the richest, largest, and most dominant political party in India. is expansion was made possible by the foundations that were laid following the party's rst electoral defeat in the 1984 general polls. e party then decided to abandon the ideals of positive secularism and Gandhian 1 socialism that it had adopted in its inception in 1980, under the leadership of Atal Bihari Vajpayee who would later serve as prime minister. In the late 1980s and the 1990s, the 2 BJP went back to the Hindutva ideology of its 3 precursor, the Bharatiya Jan Sangh (BJS). In the 1984 elections, the BJP won only two Lok Sabha seats, provoking serious introspection within the party and its ideological parent, the Rashtriya Swyamsevak Sangh (RSS). e electoral failure was seen as proof that the moderate policy of Vajpayee would not work. Vajpayee was replaced as BJP president by Lal Krishna Advani, who promptly revived the BJS's hard-line Hindutva 4 as the core ideology of the party. Advani used the Hindutva rhetoric of pseudo secularism and Muslim appeasement to great in winning popular support among the Hindus, 5 aided by the soft-Hindutva politics the Indian 6 National Congress played then. e next logical step was to join the RSSbacked Vishwa Hindu Parishad (VHP) which was leading the Ramjanmabhoomi movement. Soon, Advani became the face of a countrywide campaign to build a Ramjanmabhoomi temple in Ayodhya where the Babri masjid once stood. e hardline Hindutva politics paid rich electoral dividends in the next general elections in 1989 when the BJP won 85 7 Lok Sabha seats. In the 1991 general elections, it increased its strength to 120 and its vote share went up to 20.1 percent from 8 11.4 percent in 1989 and 7.4 percent in 1984. In the 1996 general elections, the BJP's seats in Lok Sabha went up to 161 and it staked claim to form the government as the single largest party, which was accepted. us, the rst ever BJP-led government was formed under the leadership of Vajpayee but it lasted for only 13 days as it failed to garner the support of other non-Congress, non-Left political parties to muster a majority. Vajpayee resigned, rather than face a vote of condence 9 in Parliament. In the next general polls in 1998, the BJP obtained 182 seats in the Lok Sabha and formed a coalition government called the National Democratic Alliance (NDA), which lasted 13 months from 19 March 1998 to 17 April 1999 when it lost a no-condence motion by a single vote. thereafter, in September-October 1999, the BJP-led NDA won 270 seats in the general elections, with the BJP once again getting 182 seats. Vajpayee became prime minister for the third time and his government lasted the full term until the next general polls in 2004. THE BJP'S RISE: A CONFLUENCE OF FACTORS e BJP's rise to power can be attributed partly to Advani's organisational skills, as well as the party's return to the Hindutva agenda while keeping the liberal image of Vajpayee alive in popular memory. What further helped the party was the fact that the electorate wanted a change from the long years of Congress rule. Slogans like Party with a dierence and an appeal to the electorate to give the BJP a chance captured the condence of the electorate. A little over six years of the Vajpayee government, between 1998 and 2004, established the party as a credible alternative to the Congress. However, the BJP-led NDA lost the next two general elections due to various factors, making way for a Congress-led coalition, the United Progressive Alliance (UPA), to run the government until a series of scams, high ination and unemployment and policy paralysis grounded it in the 2014 elections. is time, the BJP was led by Modi, a four-time chief minister of Gujarat and the party's prime ministerial candidate. He managed to capitalise on the popular discontent against the UPA government and won the party a majority, on its own, in Lok Sabha. The last time a party had won a majority on its own was when the Congress won 404 seats in the 1984 elections that followed the assassination of Indira Gandhi. Ever since Modi became prime minister on 26 May 2014, the BJP has been working like a well-oiled electoral machine. It has won one state election after another and is dominating the national discourse like no other party has done in recent memory. Modi-Shah Partnership e rise of Modi has also marked the rise of Amit Shah as BJP president. Rajnath Singh, who headed the party in the run-up to the 2014 electoral victory, reportedly wanted to continue in the post and stay out of the government. But this was not acceptable to Modi as that could have meant a dual power centre. Rajnath Singh had an excellent rapport with the RSS and that is why Modi did not want him to continue. e name of party General Secretary J P Nadda, a politician from Himachal Pradesh, was brought into contention and the RSS was agreeable to him. e move was made to juxtapose Shah against Nadda. Modi resolved it by inducting Singh and Nadda into his cabinet and appointing Shah, his old and trusted colleague 10 from Gujarat, as party president. is was an exception to the long-held convention that the prime minister and the party president should come from dierent states. Shah has galvanised the party, bringing in a certain ruthlessness and unprecedented administrative acumen in the way the organisation is run. It is said that his party colleagues are more in awe of him than 11 admiring. Upon taking charge, Shah introduced many changes in the party's administrative style and structure. He modernised the party set-up and developed a system that rewards individuals who deliver. He ushered in a corporate-style system of vertical heads for programmes, in contrast to the horizontal nature of the party 12 under the previous presidents. For Shah and the party, elections are nothing less than war. His advice to party colleagues after taking charge was: Elections are to be fought with clarity of mind and with the 13 single objective of victory. He enjoys the total support of Modi, stands rm in his decisions and brooks no interference from any leader. By most accounts, he has a no-nonsense style of leadership, and keeps a tight schedule and long hours of work, inspiring his team to follow 14 suit. Shah has also developed closer working relations with the RSS, as a result of which the RSS leadership and functionaries are playing a 15 bigger role in running the oganisation. In 2013, the BJP was in power in ve states Gujarat, Madhya Pradesh, Rajasthan, Chhattisgarh and Goa and was sharing power with ally JD(U) in Bihar and Shiromani Akali Dal (SAD) in Punjab. Its political fortunes have changed dramatically since then. By May 2018, the BJP, either on its own strength or with its alliance partners, was ruling in 21 of the 31 states and union territories, expanding to the regions and states where it was never in power before. In 15 states, it has its own chief ministers and in the other six, it shares power with its allies (Bihar, Jammu and Kashmir, Andhra Pradesh, Meghalaya, Nagaland and Sikkim.) In ve out of the 15 states where it has its own chief ministers, it does not have a majority of its own (Maharashtra, Assam, Jharkhand, Manipur and Goa). Since then, two states have fallen o the map TDP pulled out of the NDA leading to break in partnership in Andhra Pradesh, and BJP pulled out of the coalition governments in Jammu and Kashmir. In 2013, the BJP wrested power in Rajasthan, while retaining power in Madhya Pradesh and Chhattisgarh. In Rajasthan, it won convincingly with 161 seats in the assembly of 18 200 and a vote share of 45.2 percent. In Madhya Pradesh, it won 165 seats in a house of 19 230 with 44.88 percent votes. In Chhattisgarh, it repeated its victory by winning 49 seats out of 20 90 with a vote share of 41.04 percent. In Mizoram, which also went to vote at the same time, it did not win a single seat despite elding 21 17 candidates and got 0.37 percent votes. Assembly elections for Arunachal Pradesh, Odisha and Sikkim were held along with the general elections in 2014. In Arunachal Pradesh's 60-member assembly, the BJP won 22 11 seats with 30.97 percent votes. It joined the government two years later in October 2016 after the President's rule was imposed and the Congress, which had won a clear 23 majority of 42 seats in 2014, was split. In Sikkim, it did not win a seat and polled only 0.7 percent of the votes but became a part of the government s ince the ruling Sikkim Democratic Front (SDF) is a coalition partner at 24 the centre. In Odisha, it won 10 seats in a 147- member assembly with 18 percent of popular 25 votes. After the 2014 general elections, assembly elections were held in Maharashtra, Haryana, J&K and Jharkhand in the same year. In Maharashtra, the BJP won 122 seats in a 288- member assembly with 27.8 percent votes while its ally Shiv Sena won 63 seats and 26 together they formed the government. In Haryana, it won 47 of 90 seats with a 33.2 percent vote share and formed its rst government in the state where it had been a junior alliance partner in two previous governments. In J&K, it won 25 of 87 seats (additionally, two members are nominated to the assembly), gaining the highest percentage of votes (23 percent), with a majority of the 28 seats coming from the Jammu region. It joined hands with the People's Democratic Party (PDP), which had won 28 seats, to form a coalition government. In June 2018, the BJP pulled out of the coalition and the Governor's 29 rule was imposed. In Jharkhand, the BJP won 37 of 81 seats, 30 falling a few seats short of the majority. A coalition government was formed with the All Jharkhand Students Union (AJSU) and Raghubar Das, a party leader, became the rst from a non-tribal community to head a government in the state. In 2015, the BJP tasted defeat in the assembly elections of Delhi and Bihar. In Delhi, it could win only three of 70 seats, though 31 polled 32.19 percent of votes. In Bihar, it faced the united opposition from the RJD, JD (U) and Congress, winning only 53 of 243 seats with 32 23.42 percent votes. In 2016, the BJP won the Assam elections and formed its own government for the rst time in the state, while failing to make much headway in Kerala, Puducherry, Tamil Nadu and West Bengal. In Assam, it won 60 of 126 33 seats with 29.8 percent votes. In Kerala, it won one seat, though it improved its vote share by 34 winning 10.6 percent votes. In the Union Territory of Puducherry, it failed to win any 35 seat while polling 2.4 percent votes. e West Bengal elections were disappointing too. It could win only three seats while polling 10.28 36 percent votes. In 2017, the assembly elections were held in Goa, Manipur, Punjab, Uttarakhand, Uttar Pradesh, Gujarat and Himachal Pradesh. e BJP formed the government in Goa and Manipur despite not being the single largest party and came to power in Himachal Pradesh, Uttarakhand and Uttar Pradesh convincingly. In Goa, the BJP won 13 seats in a house of 40 while registering the highest percentage of 37 votes at 32.5. In Manipur, it won 21 of 60 38 seats with 36.3 percent votes. It wrested power from the Congress in Himachal Pradesh by winning 44 seats, out of 39 68, with a vote share of 48.8 percent. In Uttarakhand, it won 57 of 70 seats with a 46.5 40 percent vote share. In Uttar Pradesh, it registered an unprecedented victory by winning 312 of 403 seats and registered 39.67 41 percent of votes polled. In Punjab, where it was a junior partner of the SAD led government, it could win only three of 117 seats while polling 5.39 percent 42 votes. e party retained Gujarat but its tally was the lowest in the last two decades. It won 99 seats out of 182 though it polled 49.59 43 percent of votes. In 2018, the BJP registered a landmark victory in Tripura, ending 25 years of CPI(M) rule by winning 35 seats in a 60-member 44 assembly and polling 43.0 percent votes. In Meghalaya and Nagaland, however, its electoral performance was below expectations. It won two seats in a 60-member assembly in 45 Meghalaya with 9.63 percent votes and 12 of 46 60 seats in Nagaland with 15.3 percent votes. In Karnataka, it emerged as the single largest party with 104 seats in a 224-member 47 assembly while polling 36.2 percent votes. However, it failed to form the government as the Congress and JD(S) joined hands to claim a majority . BJP has been able to expand its political base in the country because of various factors including superior electoral strategies, planning, hard work, and a voter outreach programme that was far better than those of its rivals. Under the leadership of Prime Minister Narendra Modi and BJP president Amit Shah, the party devised electoral strategies taking into account micro details of caste, sub-castes, religious compositions and other specics of the constituencies while selecting party candidates. Under them, electoral victory at 48 any cost became the driving force of the BJP. Under the Modi-Shah leadership, the party was turned into a mass-based party from a 58 cadre-driven one. e BJP launched its membership drive asking citizens interested in joining the party to give a missed call on a dedicated phone number; they were then registered as members and their personal and professional details were taken. By 2015, the BJP had become the biggest political party in the country and the world, surpassing the Communist Party of China in membership 59 when it crossed 8.8-crore mark. Soon the 60 membership breached the 10-crore mark. e BJP also began to penetrate into the rural countryside, focusing on reaching the backward castes and the poor. e party paid attention to castes, sub-castes and social groups that have been neglected by other parties

Modi government has delivered upon its pre poll promise of "Minimum government Maximum governance" by taking reform measures in every sectors to streamline the governance in the country. this reformative style of governance has touched every sector from finance to Aviation and has been of every kind from being administrative to behavioral. After succeeding to a paralyzed economy, all the indicators of development and governance today speak for success of the reforms undertaken by Modi government in this short span..